Upside Down

America in Trouble 2024

Michael L. Roeder

Omni Publishing Co.
2024

Copyright @ 2024

By Michael L. Roeder

All rights reserved,
including the right of reproduction
in whole or in part in any form.

Published by Omni Publishing Co.
www.omni-pub.com

Cover Design: Dave Derby
www.DerbyCreative.com

Library of Congress cataloging in publication data
Roeder, Michael L.

Upside Down: America in Trouble 2024

ISBN: 979-8-218-39926-9

Dedication

To My Wife, Catherine. Our children and their spouses, Catharine, Christopher and Renee, Neil and Connie, and our grandchildren, Jack-Riley, Kyle, Meghan, Malia and Caeden.

How fortunate I am to have you in my life.

Author Information

This first time author is a native of Westfield, Massachusetts. He was educated in local schools and graduated from Westfield State College in 1966, the same year he joined the Massachusetts Army National Guard. He was commissioned a Second Lieutenant, Medical Service Corps, in 1969. From 1969-1983, he served in several company level command and battalion staff positions.

Mr. Roeder's professional career included fifteen years as a Connecticut State Probation Officer and program manager in that state's Judicial Department.

In 1983, as a member of the U.S. Army Reserve (USAR), he went on active duty and served in a number of medical battalion and brigade staff positions which included a tour in Saudi Arabia during Operation Desert Storm-1990-91. He went on to serve as a staff officer in the United States Army Reserve Command (USARC) in Atlanta, GA and then with the Army Surgeon General's office in Falls Church, VA. He retired from active duty in 1997 with the rank of Lieutenant Colonel.

Mr. Roeder then served ten years in the Connecticut Department of Corrections as a program manager in charge of inmate transition services for Unified School District #1. His last position before full retirement was with the Berkshire County Sheriff's office (Pittsfield, MA) as an employment counselor. He presently serves as a volunteer/trustee with several non-profit civilian and veterans' organizations in the local community.

Mr. Roeder is married to Catherine, has three children and five grandchildren. He and his wife reside in his hometown of Westfield.

Notice

I started research for this book on November 13, 2020, in response to Donald Trump's sore loser reaction to the outcome of the November 4, 2020, election. I had developed a deep concern that Trump was somehow going to turn his loss into a win by hook or by crook. Since January 6, 2021, the date of the infamous Trump inspired attack on the U.S. Capitol, I have been doing the research necessary to present as complete a picture as I can of the issues covered in the ten chapters in "Upside Down." However, with each passing day there was new "stuff" that made yesterday's "stuff" seem obsolete and irrelevant. (So, when you see "Right now," please understand that was the situation at that time I wrote about it. Any significant changes to that situation will be addressed in either Chapter Nine, "Summary," or Chapter Ten, "Afterword." I also chose to place my personal reactions/opinions in bold, black print throughout the book.

It was a volatile situation.

-Author

Table of Contents

Prologue 1
    2006 and Beyond 3
Chapter 1: The U.S. Political System 7
    The United States Moderate Party 13
    Proposals 18
    The Nine Steps 19
Chapter 2: Immigration 25
    Legislative History 30
    The Visa Program 32
    Proposals 33
Chapter 3: The Drug Scourge 37
    Proposals 43
Chapter 4: The National Debt 49
    If a Default Occurs 50
    Proposals 53
    The Recovery Plan 54
Chapter 5: Corruption 61
    U.S. Foreign Aid Program 73
    Analysis 75
    Proposals 81
Chapter 6: Climate Change 83
    What We Are Doing 89
    Proposals 95

Chapter 7: War	97
Military Posture	102
Proposals	107
Chapter 8: The Economy	109
Chapter 9: Summary	113
Immigration	113
The Drug Scourge	118
The National Debt	120
Corruption	127
Climate Change	128
War	130
The Economy	133
Chapter 10: Afterword	135
Chapter 1 - The U.S. Political System	135
Chapter 2 - Immigration	155
Chapter 3 - The Drug Scourge	160
Chapter 4 - The National Debt	165
Chapter 5 - Corruption	168
Chapter 6 - Climate Change	176
Chapter 7 - War	183
Chapter 8 - The Economy	191

Upside Down: America in Trouble 2024

Prologue

In my 43 years of work and 79 years of living on this earth, I have had the opportunity to write a lot-information and point papers, operational plans in the Army, training manuals and brochures while employed by the State of Connecticut, research papers and program proposals- to name just a few. Writing a book, however, was not on my list of things to do until 2006 when I was hired by the Berkshire County Sheriff's Office in Pittsfield, Massachusetts as an Employment Specialist for its alternative high school, the only one of its kind in the country run by a sheriff's department. After 24 months in that position, I completed my contract and retired in 2009 at the age of sixty-five.

My primary concern was the seriousness of the drug problem in the country during those tumultuous years and the impact it was having on these students in the alternative high school program. I had seen firsthand the horrific damage heroin had done in the late sixties and seventies and continued to do along with a host of additional drugs like cocaine, prescription pills and methamphetamine. My plan was to write a book about addiction among our young. I was going to call the book "Little Johnny's March to Armageddon."

Here is what I wrote in the Prologue for that book in 2007:

"After 63 years of life on this earth and 40 + years of work, I decided to write this book. It was a culmination of everything I lived through and experienced but the motivation to do something came about because of my current role in the alternative high school program in Pittsfield. You would have thought that events like the Cuban Missile Crisis, the great

Cold War, JFK's assassination and all the other assassinations, the big city riots, the corrupting power of the Mafia and other crime organizations, or the destruction of our great cities in the sixties to the heroin trade, the pervasive power of the cartels, or the Vietnam War would have provoked a guy like me to write something, even a paltry 'Letter to the Editor' but I did not."

"You would have thought that the dark days of the seventies and eighties, with runaway inflation and rampant unemployment, or the oil embargo, the Iran Hostage Crisis, 3 recessions, Watergate, the Persian-Gulf War (which I fought in), the pedophile priest debacle in the Roman Catholic Church and the HIV epidemic, might have done the trick but it did not."

Instead, an unfinished book sat on a shelf for 16 years. Nevertheless, this old Prologue is still very relevant because the issues I am writing about now are still relevant today-drugs, corruption, the economy, war, with a few more issues added- our current political system, immigration, the national debt, and climate change. These are the central issues I believe are on the verge of collapsing this country and if we go down the world will follow. You certainly have your own priorities and opinions.

There is another paragraph in the old Prologue I want to present. It describes who "Little Johnny" is in the book narrative. The description is more applicable to today's younger generations than ever before, not only in the U. S. but the world over. Credit the Great Pandemic, the media, the I-phone, our permissive culture, drugs, broken families, add your own. The question is: What are we going to do about it now? Something must be done NOW!!!

Little Johnny

"A male or female U. S. citizen, between the ages of 15-19, the product of poverty (although many in Pittsfield are not), from a broken home (many are), doing poorly in school (most do), diagnosed with a condition-Attention Deficit Disorder (ADD), Attention Deficit

Hyperactive Disorder (ADHD), Obsessive Compulsive Disorder (OCD), Social Anxiety Disorder, Sociopathic (some are), depression, dyslexia, pure anger, hostile to authority, socially maladjusted, deficient in basic comprehension, reading, mathematics, and spelling skills, poor hygiene, sexually permissive, and in a drug abuse profile (many are)."

2006 and Beyond

In 2009, I retired after 43 years of employment. My wife, Cathy, had retired by this time as well with 40 years of total employment which included 25 years with the U. S. Postal Inspection Service. Our retirement house was built and moved into. I felt a sense of full responsibility for this property as well as managing our investment properties because Cathy had done a superior job managing all of it while I was away on active military duty. Still, it was really a big pain in the ass. I had to go to court for a tenant eviction only once and won but there was always something to do, someone to go after. I would not be a property investor/owner today under any circumstances. Landlords do not stand a chance. COVID, the courts and the federal government forever changed the way that game was played.

On the world stage, 2000-2003 saw the Apocalypse in Africa, South America, Europe, especially Eastern Europe, Central America, another war in Iraq, war in Afghanistan (20 years). On September 11, 2001, the U. S. was attacked by terrorists from Saudi Arabia. It was the Pearl Harbor of the 21st century. Thousands died, the Twin Towers in New York collapsed, the Pentagon was hit with significant military casualties and damage and a civilian airliner was crashed in a field in Pennsylvania with no survivors. I was shocked, then angry, then horrified and wanting revenge. President Bush took care of that by sending our troops into Afghanistan for a quick victory against the Taliban. This country then stationed troops there for the next 20 years spending over a trillion dollars to shore up one of the most corrupt governments in the history of governments. In that process, we suffered 2,402 U.S. servicemen and women killed and another 1,921 wounded. God bless our military heroes.

From 2005-2023, things just got worse, much worse. The worldwide economic recession of 2008 and the collapse of the U. S. housing and banking markets brought long term havoc on American society and business. "Right now," U.S. banks of all types, collectively, have paid over forty-two billion dollars in fines and penalties as punishment for the massive fraud they committed. Hardly any bankers went to jail. The Gulf oil spill in Florida in 2010 was one of the worst environmental disasters in this country. The Great Pandemic in 2020 crippled not only the U.S. but the entire world. It was a health disaster that took millions of lives globally, cost millions of jobs in this country alone. The economy went to its knees overnight. About everything was closed: restaurants, schools, theaters, all kinds of businesses and there was no choice. Children became isolated for long periods of time. Millions of people were working from home. I wondered if Cathy and I would survive. We both got the shots and then got COVID like everyone else. I got infected twice but came out ok. I knew several people who did not. 2020-2022 was not a pleasant time for the people of the world and the world economy took one of the biggest hits in its history. Millions and millions of people, especially children, will never be the same.

In 2016, a guy named Donald Trump ran for President of the United State and won. He beat Hilary Clinton by winning the Electoral College but lost the popular vote by several million votes. People were tired. There were big issues on the table then and Trump had a good platform I thought, and I voted for him. He took office and immediately dealt with the immigration issue which was developing into a huge "out of control" problem along our southern border. Undocumented immigrants were coming from everywhere - Guatemala, Honduras, El Salvador, Mexico, and some from Africa. "Right now," they are also coming from Haiti, Venezuela, China, Korea, Vietnam, Russia, many countries from Africa. An immigration official stated recently that undocumented immigrants are coming from over one hundred countries. Trump also took care of the military with increased pay and benefits. In just 2 years' time, the economy was booming, employment was the lowest it had been in 10 years, the stock market was booming. He streamlined the federal bureaucracy by streamlining the regulations and the regulators. We all got the Trump tax break. He was getting things done. By the time the pandemic hit in early February 2020, something had gone wrong with this man, unfortunately. He began to fight with his own people and was firing his top people daily. He called his top health guy, Dr. Anthony Fauci, an asshole over his handling of the pandemic. He downplayed COVID-19 and then he and most of his family got COVID. During his reign, he made friends with the leader of North Korea, Kim Jong Un, and nobody liked that; he praised Russia's Vladimir Putin, one of the most corrupt world leaders out there, and nobody liked that either.

Also, during his tenure, the National Debt increased to 31.4 trillion dollars, one of the smallest national debt increases in decades. "Right now," it is over thirty-three trillion dollars and growing every day because every day at the federal level we spend more money than we take in. Also, the country now has a fentanyl and xylazine drug scourge which has killed hundreds of thousands of people in the short time these drugs have been on the streets.

Biden beat Trump up in 2020. What he has done in the past 38 months and what Trump has done since he lost, represent a primary, but not the only reason I wrote this book. Biden, Trump, and the U.S. Congress are destroying this country. We are a laughingstock, and it must stop. There are major issues out there that must be addressed NOW and resolved or managed out of crisis before it is too late.

Michael L. Roeder

Upside Down: America in Trouble 2024

Chapter 1: The U.S. Political System

("Right now," is exactly Monday evening, August 14, 2023, 11:30 P.M. I am in the computer room of my home working on this very book when my wife yells in from the living room that Trump and eighteen of his friends had been indicted earlier this day on numerous state felony counts in a Georgia state court. It was a surprise to no one. The world knew it was going to happen. Make it the fourth indictment for Trump, a sinister achievement that will never be matched by a former president. I thought about it for a while and then went back to work. I had been writing and typing since 3 P. M. that afternoon. I was tired but it did register with me that Trump could not pardon any state convictions that he might endure down the road. I thought the Georgia cases would be the catalyst for his eventual imprisonment. MLR)

I have always been moderate in my political beliefs and behavior. I am in fact a registered independent voter in the State of Massachusetts. The truth is that there are more Independents registered in this state than Republicans and Democrats combined. This is also true in my home city of Westfield. The truth is that more and more people across the country are changing their political affiliation to Independent because of the mess our elected Republican and Democratic extremists in Congress have made of the democratic/legislative process which is in danger of collapse at any moment.

Occasionally, I will lean left of the center spectrum; sometimes I will lean right of the center spectrum. Most of the time, I vote on the moderate side of an issue and usually you can do that in a free society. However, what we have "Right now" is all-out woke trench warfare between the far-left Progressive Democrats, led by President Joe Biden who has the power, at least in the U.S. Senate, and hard right MAGA Republicans, led by former President Donald Trump, who want the power back.

The idea that the current president and the former president could once again challenge each other for the U.S. Presidency in 2024 is something that 70% of American voters in a recent poll preferred not to happen in any shape or form. "Right now," that is the way it looks, sadly for this country since one of them will have to win. If they do not run, they cannot win. And then there is Kamala Harris.

This is how sad the situation is.

President Joe Biden

Joe Biden had a respected 36-year career as a U. S. Senator from the state of Delaware. He was considered a moderate. He knew how to play the game and one day he was Vice-President of the United State under Barak Obama. He had a great family with some tragic outcomes (which happen in many, many families). He has survived up to now. His kid, Hunter, is in a lot of trouble and if you believe 25% of the headlines, Joe is in potentially big trouble as well. This caper is out there "Right now" every day and not only in the New York Post. In addition, there are big concerns within his own party about his mental acuity and physical stamina. Trump has made fun of Biden's mental miscues in the past but that should not surprise anyone. Does any 80-year-old really function as a 100% every day top performer in one of the highest pressure, high expectation positions in the entire world? My answer is NO. He knows he will be eighty-two when he is sworn in for his second term. He knows he will be eighty-six by the time his second term ends in 2028. This presents another problem. Any statistician will tell you that the prediction would be that Joe Biden will not complete his second term because of old age. It is called the "Cycle of Life." How sad it would be for it to end that way? This would mean that Kamala Harris, if she is his vice-president for the second term, would become the President of the United States. My answer is NO. That cannot happen and many powerful and influential Democrats agree. During her current run, she has displayed no leadership skills whatsoever. She cannot express herself so that the average person can understand her. She is flighty, unpredictable.

(Surprise, but this has nothing to do with the fact that she is a Black female. I pray every day that a competent woman of any color be nominated and elected president of this country. I believe that 50% of the political crap that goes on in the Oval Office and the U. S. Congress would cease. MLR)

Finally, and most significantly, the saddest aspect of the Joe Biden Presidency is that he let radical House and Senate Progressives take him by the throat and force on us numerous far left programs and legislative mandates. The process has made him very vulnerable with undecided voters, Independents, moderate and conservative Democrats, and voters who may decide to vote for the first time. People are fed up with their behavior, their ideas, and their attack on societal norms, and most of the legislation they have pushed on America: Inflation Reduction Act (740 billion-1.2 trillion), Student Loan Forgiveness (745 billion (estimated), Payroll Protection Program (1.2 trillion spent, 200 billion stolen by fraudsters), 600 billion increase in borrowing within one week of the debt ceiling being raised. Debt went from 31.4 trillion to thirty-two trillion dollars in one week! They had to borrow six hundred billion dollars to pay bills! As of September 19, 2023, that debt has increased to 33 trillion+ dollars!

His strength simply may be what is staring everybody in the face- the Democratic controlled U.S. Senate with a very tight U.S. House of Representatives and the votes and money these Democrats can bring to the table for his re-election.

Former President Donald Trump

"Right now," Donald Trump has been indicted four times in recent months in federal and state courts in New York, Washington, DC, Florida, and Georgia. He faces a total of ninety-one felony counts in those courts. You would hope that eventually, Donald Trump would drop out of the race out of respect for his family, supporters and especially for the good of the country. Donald Trump cares only about himself.

He is a top-grade millionaire narcissist bully. Imagine the hell his family is living through. This is the same guy that must pay 5 million dollars on order from a New York Civil Court for violating E. Jean Carroll's rights years ago. This same guy goes on national television the next day after the court award and calls the woman a whore basically and, because of that comment and other stupid remarks, he has been sued again by this woman, who will get another monetary judgment.

(On September 7, 2023, a judge ruled Trump is responsible and will face trial, but the trial will be held only to decide the additional damages to be awarded Ms. Carroll. That trial is scheduled for early January 2024. MLR).

This is the same guy who, during the 2016 Presidential Campaign, made a comment on Access Live, a syndicated live TV show, that he could grab a woman's pussy anytime he wanted because he was famous. The host of the show, a guy named Billy Bush, thought that was great news; he lost his job the next day and was never heard from again. Trump laughed it off and got away with it.

This is the same guy who thought the late John McCain, long term U. S. Senator and well-respected naval officer who spent 5 years in a North Vietnam prison, was not an American hero because he got caught fighting in a war and went to prison. Trump is an idiot.

There is a strong possibility that Trump will be facing trial in several different courts in several states in succession while campaigning for the U.S. Presidency. There is a chance "Because whatever can go wrong will go wrong" that he could be in prison, either sentenced or in jail ILO bond during the actual election and get elected!! This ILO bond thing could happen because he has such a big mouth. It could land him in jail standing before the right judge, a Democrat.

(In his current civil case in New York, the presiding judge, Arthur Engoron, has hit Trump with a total of 15,000 dollars in fines for violating a court order not to criticize court officials involved in this case. Trump has repeatedly done so. He belongs in jail for contempt of court. Trump's lawyers have challenged this court order and achieved a partial victory with a modification of the judge's order. Give this character a little more time. He will end up in jail for contempt because he cannot control his contempt. MLR)

At 78 years of age, he is also too old to be president or should be. There is some good news here. I was hoping that he might consider for his vice-presidential candidate, 68-year-old Condoleezza Rice, a Black female, well educated (3 degrees), experienced in government, George W. Bush's Secretary of State, well respected and thought of. Just a thought.

My hope is that:

1. Donald Trump realizes the damage he is doing to this country with his crazy behavior and drops out of the race. "Right now," there are eight other candidates running for the Republican nomination. Surely, at least one of them would be accepted as a legitimate candidate. How

about Nikki Haley from South Carolina, Sen. Tim Scott from South Carolina, or Florida Governor Ron DeSantis for starters.

(Since the Republican campaign started, there have been changes. It is difficult to keep up to date, but I am doing my best. Now, in mid-November 2023, there are only 5 Republican candidates running. Soon, there will be three. On the Democratic side, Robert Kennedy, Jr. has gone Independent. Kennedy will draw votes from both the Biden and Trump camps. Cornel West is also running as an Independent. Jill Stein is the presidential candidate for the Green Party. There should be a few more Independents in the mix shortly. Time is running out. MLR)

2. Donald Trump begins to physically and psychologically fall prey to the pressures of the campaign and all the court appearances and trials, as well as the costs, estimated "Right now "to be fifty-five million dollars spent and increasing daily, and drops out of the race.

3. The Republican primaries early next year do not go well for Donald Trump and the Republican Party kicks him out of the race.

4. Things go all the way to the Republican National Convention in Milwaukee, Wisconsin in 2024 where Donald Trump is rejected because delegates came to their senses.

Most pundits agree that Trump's core followers do not have the numbers to push him through to victory in November 2024, which is why it would be a disaster if he is the Republican candidate. Biden will win, probably not by much, especially if Harris is the vice-presidential candidate. Conversely, it is possible that Biden could lose this thing if Harris is his vice-presidential candidate.

5. Joe Biden, at some point before the primaries, realizes he cannot stand up physically or psychologically and does not run for a second term.

6. Kamala Harris, at some point before the primaries, realizes she is not presidential material and drops out of consideration for the vice-presidency. "Right now," Election Day is only 11 months away so we will have to wait and see. Having said that, there is an alternative to this sorry mess and that is a well-financed third party candidate.

The United States Moderate Party

The title displayed above is my name for the third-party effort which I hope will happen soon. There are only 11 months until election day and the ramp up to execute a viable challenge will compel a lot of effort on the part of thousands of people nationwide and a ton of money, at least three hundred million dollars, if anyone is serious about a nationwide effort to identify third party candidates for President, Vice-President, U.S. Senate, the House of Representatives, and state governors. Administrative infrastructure will be necessary and will cost a fortune to organize. It can be done. There are wealthy people out there who could provide the financing. Super PACs can do amazing things.

Lo and behold, there is an organization based in Washington D. C. called "No Labels" that is loudly threatening to push forward a presidential candidate and slate if the political climate does not improve fast. Nancy Jacobson and former Democratic/Independent Senator Joe Lieberman of Connecticut, co-founders, vowed to nominate a bi-partisan ticket chosen from the center. She has her sights on U.S. Senator Joe Manchin (D-W. VA) and former Maryland Governor Larry Hogan to lead the ticket, but neither "Right now" has agreed to run. This is unpleasant news because, with each passing day, it becomes clearer and clearer that the race will be between two men few voters support.

(On November 10, Sen. Joe Manchin, III announced that he was not running for re-election for the U.S. Senate seat in West Virginia. His intent was to travel the country to "mobilize the middle." There

is already great speculation on both sides of the aisle that he will be a candidate for the No Labels Party sooner than later. MLR)

This is what No Labels believes: "A common sense majority. A national movement of people who believe in America and in bringing our leaders together to solve our toughest problems."

(I am 150% ok with that. MLR)

Also, they have constructed an insurance plan (strategy) that would allow a "Unity Ticket" to run in the 2024 election if the two main party candidates are not supported and/or the two candidates continue to be in the news for all the wrong reasons. As recently as July 17, 2023, the organization held a town meeting at St. Anselm College in Manchester, NH where they presented its "Common Sense" platform. It is a comprehensive 30-point policy platform that also contains the insurance plan.

U.S. Senator Joe Manchin, III was there as was Jon Huntsman, former Republican Governor of Utah, Larry Hogan, former Governor of Maryland, and U. S. Senator Kyrsten Sinema (I-AZ). Manchin may be the presidential candidate and Hogan or Huntsman may run for the VP slot. Nobody has committed just yet but, despite that reality, the organization has scheduled a No Labels Party convention in Dallas, Texas April 14-15.

(The convention has since been cancelled. What are you waiting for? MLR)

This organization believes our country is on the wrong track. It has been on a path to get politically recognized so far in ten states which include Arizona, Colorado, Oregon, Maine, Alaska, Nevada, North Carolina, and Florida. I acknowledge there are not a lot of electoral votes in those states. It must do more if it is serious. Otherwise, the effort will end up as a Ross Perot like spoiler in 1992 and one of the two candidates no one wants will get in anyway.

On a positive note, Jacobson wants to get on the ticket in all fifty states. "Right now," No Labels has an application pending in Wisconsin, an important "swing" state and several others. This is more like it.

(After all is said and done, that ballot number is now at 12 with several more applications pending. The party will not get on all fifty state ballots since sixteen states and the District of Columbia require a slate. An announced slate would make a big difference. MLR)

I am all in on this organization, but I do not like the party name. No Labels needs some work. I like the United States Moderate Party. It has a more centrist sound. Perhaps Jacobson will consider a change if things get rolling soon.

Whether she does or not, one thing is for certain-she must get going-fundraising, organization, management and getting commitments now is paramount. Her fundraising goal is seventy million dollars. You begin to realize what is at stake here, especially when you read around and discover that most Democrats are livid that No Labels is moving in this direction. They believe that this effort will draw votes away from Biden and give Trump the victory. Most Republicans think there is a strong possibility that is exactly what will happen if there are three people running for President of the United States. Anything could happen. My head is spinning most days recently. I am sad one day and angry the next.

After you consider everything "Right now," even though many will argue that it is still early, how many more indictments can Trump endure and how much longer can the country endure an old man under an enormous black cloud?

(I want to say this: "We deserve better than the political/social crap we are getting now, and we deserve better quality candidates for President and Vice-President of the United States. Personnel upgrades in the U.S. Congress are needed as well." MLR)

Regarding this so-called third-party movement, if any registered Democrat, Republican, Libertarian, Green Party or any registered voter or any citizen who has never registered to vote, is interested in showing support, go to your municipal Voter Registration Office and change your affiliation to Independent.

(And then stay tuned and watch the developments that are sure to take place in the next 11 months. MLR)

Eventually, if a third party is formed, it will have a trademark name. It could be "The No Labels Party" or it could be "The U.S. Moderate Party (USMP)" or it could be "The U.S. Independent Party (USIP);" or it could be something else entirely.

I believe that to do this movement right, three hundred million dollars would be necessary to create and initially launch a nationally focused organization that could support and finance a presidential ticket and develop a national campaign strategy to identify and support viable candidates for the U.S. Senate and U.S. House of Representatives across the country. Governor candidates would have to be the primary responsibility of state party workers and organizers. Seventy million dollars would not work. Three hundred million dollars would be a good start but only a start.

The idea that the emphasis would be on the race for President of the United States is correct. However, the important races for the Congress and the states' races for governor in 2024 cannot be ignored. Considerable effort and resources will have to be expended in all races because it makes little sense to me to put all resources into the president's race if that is all we think is necessary to change this country's direction. This must be an "all in" for any third party. What is the point of winning the presidency if the U. S. Senate is controlled by one party and the House of Representatives is controlled by another. A third party will need representation in both chambers, not necessarily majority control, for changes to take place, for legislation to process and pass. Most important, the radical elements that currently infest both parties will ideally be voted out of office to the point where they will have little if any impact on the political process in Congress. A good case in point is the tumultuous process to get a "Continuing Resolution" passed by Congress, which did occur at the very, very last second on September 30, 2023, thanks to the hard work of the House Speaker, Representative Kevin McCarthy (R-CA), who managed to get just enough House Democrats to vote for the resolution to avoid a federal government shutdown the next day, October 1, 2023, the first day of Fiscal Year 2024.

(This effort by McCarthy pissed off the radical Republicans in the House to the point where just one of them, Matt Gaetz (R-FL) made a proposal to have McCarthy ousted as Speaker and was successful. This forced the House of Representatives into recess while the Republicans attempted to elect a successor. The resolution funds the government until the middle of November 2023. If a budget is not passed and signed off by President Biden by that time, another Continuing Resolution will be necessary or the government will shut down, right in time for the holidays. In addition, Donald Trump was one of a dozen individuals nominated for consideration as the next Speaker of the House!!! This is about as bad as it can get for the American people. In the meantime, no business can be conducted in the House which means no budget items can be discussed and voted upon. In mid-November 2023, a second Continuing Resolution was passed and signed by the president. The new Speaker of the House, Mike Johnson (R-LA) pulled off a deal by convincing a number of Democrats to support the resolution. This angered a number of MAGA loving Republicans, which means that Johnson's days as the House Speaker are numbered. MLR)

What makes it all happen is money. And there is plenty of it around in this country. There are billionaires out there who are as disgusted as you and I are about the politics in play. "Right now," one Political Action Committee (PAC) could make all the difference. Fortunately, the organizers of No Labels are currently hard at work making a third-party movement a reality. Time is of the essence.

(Today, Monday, August 21, 2023, Donald Trump agreed to post a 200, 000-dollar bond on his Georgia state felony cases and will turn himself in to Georgia authorities by Friday, August 25th. There will be strict rules he has to follow, or he could end up in jail for bail violation. Today, the polls show Republicans giving him a 62% edge over all the other Republican candidates. With each new indictment his ratings increase! Ron DeSantis and Nikki Haley are way off in Trump's dust. This is disgraceful. The hard right faction of the Republican Party is making a mockery of democracy in this country. MLR)

If Donald Trump wins in 2024, whether he has control of both houses, one house or no houses, he will spend four years and millions of taxpayer dollars seeking revenge. The country will be a laughingstock and every American will suffer the consequences.

If Joe Biden wins in 2024, we can expect more of the same as we have seen the first three years of his reign: many civilian and military missteps, big spending programs, more national debt, declining military recruitment and readiness, more woke crap, more inflation, more taxes, more social interference, and a continuing lack of cooperation with Republicans.

Proposals

If a third party is not operational by the end of 2023, then the Republican candidates still campaigning should join forces, select one presidential and one vice-presidential candidate and launch a direct challenge to Donald Trump. Collectively, their numbers could make a difference in the mindset that is out there among us now.

(People cannot believe what is happening in this country in the political realm. Trump will prevail at the Republican National Convention if no major changes occur by the year's end. This country is in great danger. MLR)

This is why. Many years ago, Keith M. Alber, a retired judge, while in college, took a political science class on the "steps necessary to overthrow a democracy." The nine steps covered here are completely relevant in our current social and political structure, a reality that is frightening to accept as fact. With political extremists in control of our government and extremists trying to gain control, we live in perilous times, and we must never forget January 6, 2021.

The Nine Steps

Divide the nation philosophically: This has never been truer today. It is the hard right against the hard left with little representation for most moderates and conservatives in the middle of the political spectrum. The 2024 election, if it stands up the way it is "Right now", will only make matters worse, no matter who wins the presidency. Only huge changes in the composition of the U. S. Congress could reduce the political friction and allow the smooth operation of the federal government, something we have not seen in years. Our votes can make a historic difference here. This is the biggest challenge we face as a nation "Right now."

Foment racial strife: This is a done deal big time in this country-rogue police officers took care of this issue at the expense of a lot of innocent people and all the honest, unbiased police officers out there. Police brutality, aimed at mostly minorities, is a daily event in our culture and has fostered a "Defund the Police" effort by groups like "Black Lives

Matter," itself a corrupt organization, and politicians screaming for retribution and reduced police budgets. Minorities are demanding change which will not come easy, but it must come. The recent Supreme Court decision knocking out race (Affirmative Action) as a consideration for admission to college does not help matters and comes at a really bad time for race relations stability in this country.

Distrust of police authority: Abuse by law enforcement, which reached new heights of depravity in 2020 and continues to this day, has fostered not only distrust but disrespect as well in minority communities and it will take years for the many reforms taking hold "Right now" to reverse that attitude. Better hiring practices, better vetting, better training, better pay and benefits, and less nepotism in the hiring of police officers must occur at all levels of government, especially at the county level, or the country will remain in danger of never-ending displays of civil unrest and demonstrations.

Swarm the national borders indiscriminately and illegally: If something is not done immediately, the nationwide immigration crisis we are in "Right now" will morph into a national disaster socially, economically, and politically. The Biden administration, driven by left wing progressive furor, has allowed three million+ un-vetted undocumented immigrants into our country in just the last three years, to join the 12-15 million undocumented immigrants already here. There must be a final number agreed upon before we shut down our borders, especially our southern border, which is under attack day after day after day. What is the final number-15.8 million, 17.3 million, 19.6 million? Three cheers for legal immigration!

Engender the military strength to weaken it: In 2022, not one military service met its recruitment goals, including for the first time in 40 years, the United States Air Force (USAF). In 2023, all the services will again fall dramatically short of their recruiting goals. Military recruiters are laying the blame on woke policies forced on military leaders by the Biden Administration. Recruits do not want to be burdened by LGBTQ issues, race issues, Diversity, Equity, and Inclusion (DEI) issues and Critical Race Theory (CRT) issues. Gen Z candidates are turned off by it. Progressives could care less in their quest to reform this country and the world. This country must have a strong military presence considering the potential military challenges we are facing in Ukraine, Taiwan, North Korea, and the Middle East, especially Israel and the Palestinian conflict.

(Indeed, the surprise attack against Israel conducted by the terrorist organization, Hamas, in the Gaza Strip on Saturday, October7, 2023 has been acknowledged to have caught the Israelis completely by surprise. The death and destruction that has already taken place on both sides in just the first day of hostilities has the potential of morphing into a major prolonged conflict. Iran is thought to be a major player in this action. MLR)

Overburden citizens with new taxes: Taxes are always an issue. Most people agree that two things are inevitable-taxes and death. The era of federal and state stimulus checks/bonus surplus refunds is over. Massachusetts, a year ago, sent bonus surplus checks to most residents and no one complained. My wife and I certainly did not. This will change in the short term (overnight) if the federal government continues to spend money it does not have. The federal budget deficit for FY 2023 is estimated to be 1.5 trillion dollars. This is unacceptable and will lead to higher federal tax rates for the average family during a time of inflation, high interest rates, and spiraling fuel and food prices.

Encourage civil rioting and discourage accountability for all crime: There is little difference between the civil rioting back in 2020 and the protests that are occurring "Right now" for abortion rights, LGBTQ recognition, union contracts, and the like. People involved are expressing their passion for a particular idea or ideal. In the case of the police brutality incidents, people were pissed off and took out their anger on the nearest community. The January 6, 2021, attack on the U.S. Capitol was a different story altogether. It was an attack on our democracy and form of government. It was beyond brutal. Trump and his cronies are guilty of encouraging civil rioting and should go to jail if convicted of anything. Fortunately, over one thousand rioters have been convicted since January 6, 2021, and many more will be arrested and convicted. The federal courts will be in session for another three to five years, perhaps longer. Unfortunately, in many states' criminal courts, especially the progressive courts in "blue" states "Right now," crimes against persons and property are not being prosecuted. Progressive state legislatures are lessening penalties for what they consider minor crimes. Bail is no longer allowed in many criminal courts. This approach has caused havoc in many of our biggest cities. Crime is on the rise. People are losing respect for the law. They no longer fear any penalty. We are in big trouble on this issue.

Control all balloting: Donald Trump's attempt to overturn the 2020 election was really a full-blown assault on the vote. It was an attempt to nullify an honest and open national election. It shakes me to my core that the result of this horrific act may well be that Donald Trump will be elected President of the United States in 2024. Or he may be in prison and still get elected. Or he may just be in prison. This is where we come in with our vote, which we must use to make sure he does not get elected if, in fact, he is a candidate. At the state level of government, we see attempts at subverting the nomination and election process; city council meetings are disrupted to prevent votes on controversial issues; and local PTA meetings are interrupted when special interest groups feel disrespected. We are in big trouble on this issue as well.

Control all media: In today's media, the Right is represented by the likes of Fox News and the New York Post; the Left is represented by CNBC, the New York Times and the Washington Post. In between there is media just presenting the news for the common man. The real threat to our society is our ability or inability to determine who is telling the truth. Artificial Intelligence (AI) has the potential to completely distort our ability to make sound decisions based on what we are fed by the media collectively. I do not see government suppression of the media. I do see some recent attempts by the federal government to channel or control the information available for dissemination to the public by the media. This needs to be monitored by all of us. Again, our votes may be the key here as well.

The fact is that it may not take all nine conditions to bring a country down. It may take eight or three. Nothing may ever happen even if all nine conditions exist. Nevertheless, these conditions do exist in this country "Right now," especially points 1-8.

In a July2, 2023 New York Times article, Richard Haass, president of the Council on Foreign Relations, a private American firm focused on international affairs, said:

"The most danger to the security of the world is America itself. The unraveling of the American political system means that the internal threat has surpassed the external threat." I cannot disagree. "Right now," our political system is unpredictable, unreliable and hate filled. Haass became an unaffiliated voter after January 6, 2021. "This country is going off the rails,'" he concluded.

I think the following two proposals would make sense:

- Establish term limits in the United States Congress. In the U. S. Senate, 3- six-year terms and out with a full pension; in the House, 5- two-year terms and out with a partial pension.

- Age limit on service as President and in the U. S. Congress. If one is serving and turns seventy-five, he/she is allowed to finish his term but cannot run again. When a person turns seventy-five, he/she can no longer run for the Office of President of the United States or in the Senate or the House. Something must be done. Dianne Feinstein (D-CA) passed away on September 9, 2023, at 90 years of age. President Biden will be eighty-two if he is sworn in again in 2024. Donald V. Trump is seventy-seven, Mitch McConnell(R-KY) is eighty; Nancy Pelosi(D-CA) is eighty-three and has announced her intention to run again in 2024; Chuck Grassley (R-IA) is eighty-nine; Bill Pascrell (D-NJ) is eighty-six; Bernie Sanders (I-VT) is eighty-one. The list of senators and representatives over eighty is a mile long. It just is not working anymore. People are fed up with this system run by a bunch of old people. I am seventy-nine and could not agree more.

Chapter 2: Immigration

"Right now," no one really knows how many undocumented immigrants are living in this country. Estimates range from eleven million-fifteen million people. I think the number is closer to fifteen million when you factor in those immigrants who snuck into the country without anyone knowing. Then you have the "Dreamers" who number about one million and then you must include the millions of people who came into this country on a visitor's visa and simply never returned home. In 2006, 45% of undocumented immigrants in this country were Visa overstays. Add a few million more.

Consider the incredible numbers crossing into this country. "Right now," the figures for calendar year 2023 will total out close to 2 million+ new undocumented immigrants, many of them children and many children and adults needing health care and social services indefinitely. And then there are the "Gotaways," estimated by the government to number 1.2 million.

This country's immigration system has collapsed, albeit in slow motion, over the past three years. Under Biden, it has become a daily, tragic horror show at our southern border and across this country as hundreds of thousands of undocumented immigrants are shipped to unprepared, under-staffed and under-financed cities despite pleas for help from governors and big city mayors from New York, Chicago, San Francisco, St. Louis, Washington D.C., Atlanta, and Philadelphia, just to name a few. Leadership from Congress on workable immigration legislation has been lacking for the past 25 years. Congress has not had the political will to submit one piece of legislation to the Office of The President since 2006. We are paying the price for it now.

Donald Trump deserves every negative comment sent his way about his recent past and present behavior. Nevertheless, in his first two years in office, 2017-2018, he had immediate impact on the immigration problem when huge masses of immigrants were marching from Central America - Guatemala, Honduras, and El Salvador - to join hundreds of thousands of Mexicans, all heading for El Paso, Texas. Trump told them not to come but they kept coming so he asked the leaders of the four countries to help and stop the marching. Mexico cooperated but the Central American presidents told Trump to take a long walk off a short pier. They realized that the more people that left their countries, the less social costs they would have to bear, which allowed them to steal even more government funds. Corruption is endemic in Central America- nothing is sacred.

Trump retaliated by suspending their foreign aid checks for that fiscal year. I was shocked to discover that those three little countries were scheduled to receive 750 million dollars from this country.

(More about our foreign aid program later in this book. MLR)

There is no question that Trump took a hard right on immigration when he took office, and it stayed that way during his tenure.

Almost immediately after being sworn in, Joe Biden opened the flood gates at the southern border's seventy-one checkpoints, prominently at El Paso and Brownsville, TX and San Diego, CA. In the past three years, over three million undocumented immigrants have been allowed in the country and "Right now," those numbers are increasing by the boatload every day. They are coming from over one hundred countries non-stop, but it must stop because a country that has a 34 trillion-dollar national debt that increases every day, the cost of funding this out-of-control program has the potential to cripple this country and its cities politically, socially, and financially. Federal, state, and local governments could collapse because they cannot fund the sheer numbers of undocumented immigrants showing up at their doorsteps with no resources whatsoever. The Biden Administration has created mass confusion, conflicting policies, some enforced, most not, congressional outrage from Republicans and Democrats, massive outlay of funds in the billions and ever-increasing numbers of immigrants. At the state level, those hit hard by this country-wide migration of helpless people are demanding financial help and are not getting what they need. New York City is a classic case in point. Since January 2023 over 160, 000 undocumented immigrants have been sent to the city by the State of Texas and by the Biden Administration. The city will have spent 4.3 billion dollars over the next ten months on this problem, with little monetary support from the feds or the State of New York. The city is a mess in so many ways.

What is more disconcerting is the processing, or actual lack of it, that is conducted by the U.S. Border Patrol on the undocumented immigrants it does arrest. Over 1.6 million undocumented immigrants have been allowed in this country since January 2023. The majority have not been vetted, no background checks completed, no medical exams conducted, nothing. They have been given court dates for their asylum hearings that may be up to five years distant. In the Boston, MA Federal Immigration Court there are presently 177,000 immigration cases pending. More cases are added to the docket every week. There are 1.6 million asylum cases pending in this country "Right now." In 95% of all those cases, the client will not show up. Nothing will happen and nothing has been happening for years. The undocumented immigrant disappears into the heartland forever.

(This means that the client lives in the underworld, earning low wages under the table, unable to grow and prosper. He is abused, his rights are violated, the family lives in abject poverty. What an ugly

system. What would you expect? I am describing the undocumented system of immigration that operates in this country within a mostly legal framework. MLR)

Congress is the key to significant change. The Executive Branch (Trump, Biden) will always react to an issue and issue directives and policies as both have. Trump policies were aligned to the conservative side and pushed way to the right in a short period of time. Biden was elected and immediately reversed many of Trump's immigration policies by Executive Order. Overnight, the shift went way to the left.

This is what Trump wanted to do in 2017, when he took office:

- He wanted a 2000-mile border wall to be built and got five hundred miles built before his first and only term ended.
- He banned travel to majority-Muslim countries.
- He wanted to end birthright citizenship. (unsuccessful)
- He wanted no permanent residency granted to undocumented immigrants likely to need welfare assistance. (unsuccessful)
- He proposed prohibiting U. S. citizens from bringing in non-citizen relatives. (denied by Congress)
- He used Title 42, part of the U.S. Health Code, which allowed the government to immediately deport illegal immigrants arrested at our borders. (Used legally to deport millions during COVID, 2020-2023.)

This is what Biden wanted to do when he took office in January 2021:

- Stopped funding for the border wall. (successful)
- Travel bans to Muslim countries rescinded. (successful)
- Ended Title 42 in July 2023. (successful)

- Established new immigration policies after 5/11/2023 but enforcement has been erratic under Title 8, the policy manual that was in force prior to the implementation of Title 42.
- Let in a ton more people. In 2022, 2.4 million will be admitted in our country; 1.6 million since January 2023, and an estimated 1.2 million "gotaways" that the Border Patrol did not catch.
- Implemented a policy of distribution of undocumented immigrants throughout the country by plane, train, and bus at a cost of untold billions of federal and state dollars since 2021. (successful but not really)

The press, liberal and conservative, have had a field day on this issue. One journalist, Nicole Gelinas, of the New York Post, in an op-ed piece published on August 2, 2023, had some very relevant questions about the President Biden's immigration policy:

1. What is your immigration and asylum plan?
2. What is your plan to ensure that undocumented immigrants will show up for their asylum court hearing since the majority will not be granted asylum in the first place?
3. What is your plan to clear a years long backlog of 1.6 million asylum cases?
4. What is your plan for most applicants who won't qualify for asylum?

Three of the four questions concerned the court process which has been broken for years. It is shameful. The first question is the big one and for that question and all four, there have been no answers forthcoming, and we are into Biden's third year in office. Only chaos can come of all this. Congress must do something now, but it is unlikely if the past is any indication.

Legislative History

In the past seventeen years, nothing in the form of legislative action has happened in Congress with immigration policy although several attempts were made, all futile. It was a matter of political animosity, rivalry, and lack of will.

Whatever it was then, it is one thousand times worse today in the Congress. It is an uncommon event when any type of legislation passes.

Since 2006, various legislative proposals were presented in Congress but not one passed. Some did come close.

In 2006, the Republican led Senate passed the Comprehensive Immigration Reform Act by a 62 to 36 vote. The Act called for security improvements to the border, more border agents, a pathway to citizenship for undocumented immigrants, and a guest worker program. The bill died when the House refused to consider the bill.

In 2007, with new Democratic majorities in the Senate and the House, the Senate majority put forth a bill that proposed improved security measures to include radar, fencing, aerial surveillance, 24,000 additional border agents, and a pathway to legal status based on points for skills, education, family ties, and English proficiency for undocumented immigrants living in the United States. The bill never got a vote in the Senate.

In 2010, Democrats failed to carry the "Dream Act" which sought to give young migrants a chance for legal status. On December 10, 2010, the House passed the bill. Ten days later, a Senate vote fell five votes short of breaking a filibuster. Thirteen years later, the bill has not passed.

In 2013, the Senate passed a bill, 68-32. The House defeated it. House Speaker John Boehner refused to bring it to the floor for a vote. The bill addressed security upgrades, a 13-year pathway to citizenship,

E-Verify, an employment eligibility system to control immigration, a VISA system based on points, and a guest worker program.

In 2018, a divided Republican Senate killed a proposed "Dreamers" bill that included a 13-year pathway to citizenship, stepped up border security, and a host of unpopular, very conservative rules that killed the chance of passage. Trump played a crucial role in its demise.

In April 2023, legislation was presented in the House of Representatives by the Republican majority. It provides funding for the southern border Wall, several thousand additional Border Patrol (BP) officers, payment of retention bonuses to BP employees, advanced technology purchases, and the elimination of the CPB1 APP used now by undocumented immigrants applying for asylum. This APP is twelve pages and is a bear to complete. It is also a major reason undocumented immigrants try to sneak into the country. The legislation has little chance of passage.

So far in this century, Congress has not put an immigration bill before the President of the United States. Inaction has led to immigrant abuse and exploitation, a huge backlog of asylum cases, enrichment of cartels through drug smuggling, uncertainty at the border on both sides of the fence, and huge unplanned and unbudgeted expense at all levels of government that is estimated to have cost U.S. taxpayers 200 + billion dollars since Biden took office.

Michael L. Roeder

The Visa Program
(US Department of State)

If I ever saw a program that needs major reform the U.S. VISA Program, is it. I am hardly the expert in this area, but I have done considerable research to learn as much as I could and then combine it with what I know from extensive readings on the problems existing "Right now" with the Green Card application process and the H-1B VISA foreign immigrant employment process in this country.

An immigrant seeking to enter the United States must obtain a VISA which is then placed in that person's passport. There are two main categories of US VISAs- Non-immigrant for temporary travel into the country and Immigrant to live permanently in this country. When a visiting immigrant does not leave the country on time, he becomes "out of status." In the worst case he will be ineligible for a VISA in the future. That is the extent of it. More severe penalties need to be imposed. At the very least, an effort should be made to locate the immigrant for return to his country of origin but that is not happening. I was unable to get a number of immigrants who have failed to depart this country. Not even an estimate. This could involve several hundred thousand people, perhaps several million, living in this country illegally.

The Green Card is a permanent resident card that allows a non-citizen immigrant to live and work permanently in this country. The card is awarded from a lottery which an immigrant enters after completing an involved application. Millions apply annually. There are ten other ways to get a Green Card. Immigrants first complete a VISA application and enter the country after completing a Green Card application. The Immigrant VISA allows employment in the H-1B category. It can take years for an immigrant to get a Green Card. It is an administrative nightmare that must be corrected.

In a New York Times article dated December 10, 2022, Miriam Jordan wrote a heartbreaking story involving a Green Card applicant from India who had been working at Microsoft in Bellevue, WA since 2008. He was an experienced engineer, married with two children. He was earning a six-figure salary, owned a beautiful home. Life was good until he got laid off in October 2022 during the employment wipe out that hit the IT industrial complex that year. He was authorized to work with the issuance of a work visa way back in 2008. He had been waiting for his Green Card since 2013. His work Visa was under the H-1B category. Abshi was on the cusp of securing permanent US residency. Now, he is facing deportation and must leave the country with his family in 60 days unless he finds employment and another sponsor. His employer gave him an excellent severance package. He said Microsoft was a good employer. If he gets another job, his new employer will have to shell out $20,000 for an H-1B waiver and green card fees. There are currently 500,000 H-1B employees in this country. Most are from India and China. In 2022 U.S. employers filed more than 480,000 petitions for the 85,000 H-1B visas available annually. A lottery decides who gets picked. In Abshi's case, there is a happy ending, sort of. On December 22, 2022, he got his Green Card in the mail, totally unexpected. He is still looking for work but is now a permanent resident. There are currently nine million permanent residents eligible for US citizenship. From 1995-2019, 22.1 million immigrants became citizens. In 2022, 970,000 immigrants became citizens. I wonder now how long it will take Abshi and his family to become citizens?

Proposals

Several of these proposals are mean-spirited and lean hard to the right of the political spectrum. They are actions that Donald Trump and his radical friends would lend 110% support to. I lean to the right because time demands it. Immigration is so out of control in this country, the stringent proposals are necessary and they will work. If nothing else they will, if enacted, save this country hundreds of billions of dollars annually and prevent the kinds of social upheavals that are caused by the current onslaught of undocumented immigrants. The harshest should be easy to recognize:

- Close the borders to all immigrants for two years (except H-1B) and conduct a purge of the immigrants in this country. The "legal" system of immigration and naturalization will continue to serve immigrants who choose to become citizens legally. This purge will require the marshalling of government resources at all levels and the cooperation of the very countries which are presently doing nothing to mitigate the current calamity. If a "National Emergency" must be declared, so be it.

- "Dreamers" would be protected. Those immigrants who entered the country on visitor visas and never returned home would be easy to find and taken into custody and released when they have purchased a ticket home at their own expense. The numbers here could be quite high, a million or more. No-one really knows how many there are.

- Suspend all U. S. visa programs, except the HB-1 employment program, for one year and restructure the entire program. The current U.S. Visa program is a hodge-podge of visa categories for immigrant and non-immigrant categories that have overwhelmed the bureaucracy. Green Cards for permanent residency can take 5-10 years or more to process.

- Repeal the 14th Amendment which will end birthright citizenship for children of undocumented immigrants born in this country. In a March 3, 2018, New York Post article, Paul Sperry, way back then, highlighted the costs associated with children in this category. He claimed that the Center for Immigration Studies estimated that over the next decade, 1.7 million undocumented immigrants will enter this country. That figure was surpassed long ago, not even three years into the next decade. Future costs will cover what they cover now with taxpayer dollars-social welfare obligations, public education, food stamps, health care, housing subsidies, and the earned Income tax and child tax credits. In 2018, 62% of all undocumented immigrant heads of households were on the dole primarily because of their children born in the United States. This statistic holds true even when one or more workers are present in the household. The idea that undocumented immigrants are ineligible for welfare in this country is a cruel joke. Welfare costs for this group are out of control.

- Prohibit U.S. citizens from bringing in non-citizen relatives into the country permanently. Visits routinely turn into undocumented permanent residency.

- Finish the southern border Wall.

- Pass a "stand alone" "Dreamers Immigration Bill" to protect immigrants brought into this country years ago as children.

- Complete a comprehensive "National Immigration Bill" in twelve months' time through joint work groups in the U. S. Senate and House.

This bill should include a point system based on individual skills, education, family ties, background check for adults, English proficiency. and the needs of this country before entry is granted. Previous attempts by Congress to pass a point system have failed.

I do believe pressure from the common man (YOU AND ME) could move this issue to the forefront of the political spectrum. Action is needed now, not sometime next year or after the 2024 election. Frankly, I expect no action will be taken unless the voters in this country start getting tough with their votes, which represent the most powerful tool we have to get things moving in the direction we want.

Michael L. Roeder

Chapter 3: The Drug Scourge

To begin with, to understand my position on this terribly important subject, a few definitions are in order:

- **Drug Use:** the use of a drug to maintain health, treat health disorders like high blood pressure. In this context, drug use is a good thing.

- **Drug Abuse:** the use of a drug to get high. This is not a good thing.

- **Drug Addiction:** the use of a drug to avoid physical withdrawal or Delirium Tremors (DTs) as in the case of an alcoholic who attempts to go "cold turkey." Withdrawal from cocaine, a stimulant, may have more of a psychological than physical component. This is not a good thing.

On March 8, 1968, I reported for duty as a state Probation Officer to the 14th Criminal Circuit Court in downtown Hartford, CT, the largest criminal court in the State of Connecticut. I had been hired a month before and was now positioned after training to supervise a caseload of at least two hundred probationers, 70% who were drug addicts. They ranged in age from 17-70, but most were in their late teens, early twenties. The job changed my life and my outlook on life after a very short time working in that court. Within days of court watches and case dispositions, I could see the damage caused by heroin, a highly addictive narcotic ravaging the city, the state, and the country. By this time, I was a member of the Connecticut National Guard, so I was familiar with military affairs. I was stunned to see servicemen and servicewomen (occasionally) just back from Vietnam, appearing in the 14th CC for drug related charges. In Hartford, heroin was selling for $10 a glassine bag at 2% pure so everyone was doing the needle to get the immediate effect from the dose. Some snorted, some smoked the heroin, but needle injection (mainlining) straight into a vein was the way to go. In Vietnam, brown heroin was $2 a vile and had a purity level of 90% or higher. These soldiers were coming home thoroughly addicted with no hope of salvation. I saw it every day. If it was not heroin, it was percocet, LSD, cocaine was trending, and marijuana possession and sale cases were on the daily docket by the boatload. Most individuals were released on low bond or a Promise to Appear (PTA), which meant they were free to return to the streets to continue their criminal behavior to find the cash to buy more drugs and pay attorney fees. Eighty percent of all cases before that court were drug related day in and day out. The place was a zoo. The streets of Hartford were a zoo.

As concerning was the fact that the wealthy kids from suburbia- Avon, Simsbury, Canton, Wethersfield, West Hartford, and the University of Connecticut campus in Storrs, would come into the city to buy drugs, whether for use or sale back home, and get picked off by the police officers. It was like shooting fish in a barrel. Cops would tell me you could see them from a mile away.

How bad is it today compared to what I experienced as a Probation Officer in Connecticut in the late sixties, early seventies? The numbers tell the story. Today, heroin is sold at 40-60% pure on the street and sweetened with fentanyl (which is 50-100% more potent than morphine) and/or with xylazine (a powerful animal tranquilizer) which was stronger than anything out there in 1970. The cost depends on a number of factors like supply/demand, location, ability to deliver product, but the price "Right now" in Springfield, MA is $5 a glassine bag. Pills are big business, both the real kind like Xanax and the fake kind of Xanax, which "Right now" is more than likely fentanyl laced with xylazine, which is killing users, especially young users with low tolerance. This combination of fentanyl and xylazine is called TRANQ on the street. Even today, it is not regulated at the federal level; legislation to regulate it was submitted in March 2023, but as of August 10, 2023, it sits in front of the Senate Judiciary Committee. This lack of action is despicable. This kind of horror did not exist in the 60s and 70s. These pills and heroin and cocaine laced with fentanyl, are killing on average a 150, 000 Americans annually.

Hundreds of thousands more users, perhaps a million more users across the country, are walking around our big and small cities like zombies, completely helpless, living in tents and doorways and surviving because communities are conducting "Harm Reduction" services which allow these addicts to stay alive and do their drugs without interference. Street workers, police officers, and volunteers traverse the streets of New York, San Francisco, Seattle, Portland, Chicago, too many to list here, with kits filled with fresh crack pipes, fentanyl test strips and Narcan to treat an overdose and save lives. Interestingly enough, "Right now" Narcan does not work on Xylazine, and it often takes 2 or 3 or more doses of Narcan to reverse a heroin/ fentanyl overdose.

Illegal drug sales are on the rise in this country and the world over. The emphasis is on synthetic made fentanyl because it is much cheaper to produce than heroin and cocaine. "Right now," a fentanyl pill produced in Mexico for $.10 can sell for ten dollars a pill or more in New York City. The demand for these drugs in this country is insatiable. Law enforcement leaders have not seen anything like this ever. Despite record seizures of heroin, cocaine, fentanyl powder and pills by law enforcement agencies in recent years, the supply remains strong.

In the last two calendar years in the United States, there have been substantial local, county, state, and national seizures of all types of drugs-heroin, cocaine, fentanyl, pills of all kinds. Internationally, some of the most notorious drug kingpins in the universe have been in trouble and thrown in prison for life. Despite the heroic work by all levels of law enforcement, the supply never seems to diminish in the long run and these imprisoned thugs are replaced by even more ruthless individuals.

In a January 4, 2023, article, The Springfield Republican reported that fifteen kilos (33 pounds) of cocaine and 14,000 fentanyl pills were seized from a major drug wholesaler in Springfield, MA, a city of 150,000 people in the western part of the state. A regional task force arrested him. The haul was worth at least two million dollars retail. Two Springfield based gangs were supplied by a known drug supplier in the area. The city is a major distribution center for drugs being shipped to Vermont via Interstate 1-91, a straight shot in about an hour. Springfield Mayor Domenic Sarno, a law-and-order guy recently re-elected, publicly laments the courts and progressive judges who routinely release these crooks on low or no bonds. No need to blame law enforcement for this ugly reality. Sarno is correct when he reminds these judges that these crooks do not stop what they are doing; they get right back at it which impacts the quality of life in all communities, including Springfield.

In a January 6, 2023, article, a New York Post journalist described how in calendar year 2022, 72 million doses of fentanyl were seized in New York State-1.9 million pills and 1,958 pounds of fentanyl powder. That same year the Drug Enforcement Agency (DEA), a federal agency, seized 50.6 million fake pills laced with fentanyl and more than 10,000 pounds of the powdered drug. Most of the seizures occurred at our southern border. The article indicated that in 2022, 80% of overdose deaths in New York City, some 3,000, were caused by fentanyl. The chemical precursors for fentanyl which come from China, are shipped to Mexico for manufacture in clandestine laboratories and then shipped through one of seventy-one southern border checkpoints to places like New York City, Chicago, Phoenix and Atlanta. And the drugs keep coming by truck, train, plane, submarine (that's right submarine), private cars, shipments of drugs of all kinds from about everywhere.

The drug trade is a separate, major economy in this country and is controlled by organized crime "gangs" with connections to cartels in Mexico, Europe, Central and South America. Drug trade profits are a primary source of income in some countries like Mexico, Peru, and Columbia. The drug trade is protected by the government in some countries. Columbia, Peru, and Ecuador are good examples.

Ecuador has become a drug state in just the last 2-3 years. Drug cartels have taken over the country. The recent assassination of a presidential candidate happened because he said he would restore law and order to a country where law and order were once sacrosanct. The mafia believed he was serious, so he was killed. Happens all the time. In 2022, over 210 tons of drugs were seized coming out of the country which is located between Columbia and Peru. It is now a major transit point to the United States. There were 450 killings in Ecuador that year as well. Prisons have become centers of influence for organized crime cartels from Mexico and Albania. Street gangs have taken over entire neighborhoods throughout the country.

On August 9, 2023, fifty-one-year-old Dairo Usuga Daoip from Columbia was sentenced to 45 years in prison in New York Federal Court for importing tons of cocaine from Columbia into the United States from 2012-2022. The sentencing judge called him more prolific than the late Columbian drug-lord, Pablo Escobar. As part of the sentence, Dairo forfeited 216 million dollars. He said he was able to stay free for many years through bribery of public officials and killing a lot of people.

Where is all this taking us as a society? In 2017, Opioid overdose deaths were declared a national emergency by the Congress and President Trump. Back then, everybody already knew we had a serious drug abuse/addiction problem in this country. A major study completed and released in 2021 showed the experts may have underestimated how bad it was. I personally will not argue with this data because you must accept that a lot of research and hard work went into this report. I believe, however, that any report released "Right now" will show dramatic increases in overdose deaths from opioids, cocaine, and fentanyl especially, and significant increases in the overall numbers of users of illegal drugs. In 2021, 2 short years ago, the report identified 61.2 million people 12 and older who used an illegal drug that year, 22% of the total population; 29.5 million alcoholics drank and were designated as having Alcohol Abuse Disorder (AAD); 14.8 million people had Cocaine Use Disorder (CUD) and 1 million were addicted to the drug, Cocaine Abuse Disorder (CAD); 3 million people had Opioid Use Disorder (OUD). In 1970, most experts believed that the heroin population numbered close to one million addicts. Today that number is estimated at two million. The increases have been staggering the last 50 years or so and it is getting worse and a lot deadlier. Fentanyl has changed everything.

It does not stop here, however. Another activity that is primarily impacting our youth 10-15 years of age is Chroming, the inhaling of toxic chemicals, an extremely dangerous activity that can maim or kill. The Gen Z Generation engages in ever increasing numbers since the pandemic hit in 2020. It is a practice of inhaling aerosol from cans, paint thinner, hairspray, glue, cleaning products, and gas vapors. "Bagging" is placing a substance in a bag and inhaling the vapors and "Huffing" is using a saturated rag and placing it over the nose. Inhaling vapors and sniffing glue have been around for many decades. I saw it back in the sixties. Kids into this were often non-functional. Today the use is more frequent, and the products used can produce serious dependence, permanent brain damage and death. I mention this because it must be part of the national drug strategy, part of the solution to this so far intractable onslaught on our society.

Proposals

Anyone who thinks the scourge can be defeated and that we can lead a drug free life is completely delusional. I do think this is a problem area that can be managed to minimize the deaths and social destruction we see today, especially with the emergence of fentanyl and xylazine. The strategies are complex and must interact with each other in a sustained fashion and must be supported by huge funding, at least one trillion dollars annually, at the federal and state levels. If we can go into debt to the tune of 33 trillion dollars today, we can certainly spend a trillion dollars a year to save hundreds of thousands of lives and minimize the destruction of hundreds of thousands of families each year, not to mention the trillion dollars a year lost in economic activity in this country because of drug abuse and addictive behaviors.

- Declare a state of Martial Law in the United States and conduct an all-out war on the illegal drug establishment using all federal, state, and local law enforcement agencies under the umbrella of an enhanced federal Drug Enforcement Agency (DEA). We have this now to some degree but there is a lot of competition, lack of information sharing, turf wars that hamper the effort. Declaring a "National Emergency" would not do the trick. This type of status happens all the time and nobody knows it. The last three U. S. Presidents used a National Emergency to impose sanctions on countries that were behaving badly. Martial Law would let the world know that the game is over for us and them. The current situation demands this type of apocalyptic action.

- Make fentanyl and xylazine Category III drugs and create serious penalties for sale AND possession at the federal level and urge states to do the same.

- No plea bargaining, fines, suspended sentences, probation or parole, community service, half-way houses, ankle bracelets unless the charge is a possession without violence. And no bail, especially in drug sale cases, even simple retail sales.

- Congress must pass "The Fentanyl Eradication and Narcotics Deterrence (FEND) of Fentanyl Act" before the Congress now.

- Enact severe penalty federal legislation for the sale and mere possession of xylazine. Congress must pass "The Combating illicit Xylazine Act" before Congress now.

- Eliminate plea bargaining in all federal drug distribution and sales cases. Set maximum bonds that require 100% cash payments. No bondsman and increase prison sentences.

- Substantially increase the penalties for sale and distribution of all drugs, especially heroin, cocaine, fentanyl and xylazine. Tie possession of drugs charges into rehabilitation options rather than jail options unless violence is involved. Under a nationally coordinated strategy that starts in the federal courts with an initial appearance, conduct a mandatory drug screening for any charge, drug specific or not, to determine if drugs play any role in the criminal conduct. Options could be identified at this stage of the court processes. Arrests involving violence or the confiscation of large amounts of drugs would make the defendant ineligible for drug referral and also ineligible for bond. This type of program would work better at the state or county level courts. No matter at what level, it will cost a fortune to implement. What exists now in most court systems is an initial appearance before a judge and the imposition of no or low bond and a continuance with the defendant often released to go back on the street to commit more crime. An outcome under this system could be in-patient/out-patient treatment with the case continued before a plea is entered. This type of outcome is rare in this country's court systems. If it did become an option, the states opting to get involved and the federal court system would have to undergo major resource expansion at great cost but it would take tremendous pressure off local communities across the country, communities that are under siege from this drug driven criminal activity like never before.

A mandatory national drug curriculum starting at the seventh-grade level and continuing through high school. The educational approach now has been dependent on local and state initiatives and always subject to local fears and pressures. In some communities, the "DARE" program has been praised while condemned in others. Many liberal and conservative activists have opposed school drug education programs because the children learn all about these dangerous drugs when it is not even in their mindset. At what point do these kids need to know about the dangers of fake pills and fentanyl? If parents took the responsibility to educate their children about the dangers of drugs in their communities, I might take a different attitude. They are not because most parents would have no idea about what they were talking about. In addition, their attitude often is, "Not my kid." Today, parents are raising hell about trans gender issues, LGBTQ policies, Critical Race Theory (CRT), Diversity, Equality and Inclusion (DEI) and bus routes. All well and good, but you never read anything about parental concerns over drug education.

Repeal the 8th Amendment to the U. S. Constitution: this amendment has, since the beginning of time, stipulated that bail will be used to insure a defendant appears in court to answer charges. A repeal is a long, long, long shot. I believe that bail should exist to protect the public from the defendant, thereby ensuring the public's safety. This is especially true of people who are selling and using drugs; if they are released, 99.99 % go right back to their criminal behavior. High or no bail would prevent this, but it would place tremendous pressure on the federal prison system and those states that went along with a constitutional change as well. "Right now," in so many courts, especially state systems controlled by Progressive legislatures and judges, bail is considered a nuisance. Cash bail has been eliminated. To be arrested for shoplifting in many states, a major activity of drug addicts, you must steal over 1,000 dollars' worth of goods and if you are a security guard at a Walgreen's and you attempt to stop the theft, you might get arrested. The entire system is "upside down."

- Substantially increase border funding, for both borders and at our major airports. We need more X-Ray capability, more agents, about 20,000 to take control of seventy-one inspection stations on the southern border alone, more drug sniffing dogs, more tractor-trailer inspection stations, more of everything.

- Eliminate homeless camps that exist in about every major city in this country. Drug addicts cannot and do not pay rent because all available funds they have go to buy drugs. This includes the state and federal welfare they somehow get because they are drug addicts. Drug addicts do not work because they are too busy committing crime to get the cash they need to buy drugs. Many end up homeless and in homeless camps or "communities," a term used by the progressive elements that control the cities where the biggest homeless camps exist-New York, San Francisco, San Diego, Chicago, Portland, Seattle, the list here is endless as well. There is no national strategy in existence "Right now" to eventually put an end to this disaster. Most states have no policy either. Each city is on its own.

Each city reacts to this homeless situation depending on who is in control and how angry the locals get. This is a problem where conservatives are in control as well. No matter where a camp exists, you will see a preponderance of drug addicted people shooting up all hours of the day and night. Many of these camps are in the downtown locations of major cities. You will see people with needles stuck in their arms unconscious or dead in the middle of a sidewalk. You will see people defecating on the street in broad daylight. You will see a female giving some guy a blow job in broad daylight. You will see trash everywhere. You will see violence. It is an absolutely sickening sight. There is a solution, and it is to place these homeless people, for starters, in housing.

That will not happen "Right now" because there is no housing anywhere you go for these people. Shelters are and have been full everywhere for some time and there are long waiting lists for subsidized government housing for people not on drugs. Also, in most communities, the political will is missing, monies are not budgeted, so the problem continues to grow as more people get addicted and fall by the curbside literally and figuratively. What has happened in many communities where funds have been budgeted is a concept called "Harm Reduction."

- Eliminate Harm Reduction- this is a treatment modality that attempts to create a safe environment where drug addicts can shoot drugs without interference. Subsidized programs under contract to a municipality provide the homeless community with safe places to go to shoot up under supervision of trained medical personnel. If there is an overdose, counselors administer Narcan to save lives and they do. Addicts are provided kits containing fresh crack pipes, fentanyl swipes to test their drugs, Narcan, lip balm, health items and the like. In addition, these programs help addicts get welfare-food stamps and Medicare, cash in some states- to help. One addict was quoted in a newspaper article that the homeless community he lived in was "Paradise on earth." Harm Reduction simply means that this country will have to finance this practice and foot the bill for hundreds of thousands of addicts across the country who will never get off the drug they are on. It is costing this country hundreds of billions of dollars "Right now" and the costs are only going to increase. It is madness. What is needed are drug treatment programs for these people, then job training or employment if they have a skill, affordable housing, and government support for those who stick to it for 12 months. This will cost hundreds of billions of dollars and "So what." It is better than spending billions of dollars on a concept that will collapse under its own weight because it will be unaffordable in the long term.

(I understand that some politicians and many citizens will not support this Idea. If there is another way out of this catastrophe, fine. MLR)

Chapter 4: The National Debt

The U. S. National Debt is a game of Russian roulette we are losing. Every year we play with the debt ceiling fiasco created by an indifferent and incompetent Congress, we get closer and closer to taking that fatal bullet. We have taken this debt ceiling game to the outer limits many times in the 20th century. The last big one was during the Obama administration in 2011 when he and Congress once again went head-to-head on spending and spending cuts. Democrats always want more and Republicans less. At the last minute, an agreement was worked out, but much economic damage was done, especially on Wall Street, which went into panic over the stalemate. The one just resolved on June 3, 2023, at the very, very last second, almost sent this country and the world economy into the economic abyss. The next time it comes up in 2025, if there is not a quick agreement, we lose. If there ever is a government default on paying our debt obligations, all hell will break lose in this country and the world. "Right now," there is an agreement on spending and cutbacks over the next two years and that is a good thing, although I suspect it will not hold water. My concern is after that. We need to face the situation on new spending big time and cut back on budget allocations by fifteen percent, except for military spending, due to the world situation we find ourselves in "Right now." Ukraine has the potential for expanded warfare in Europe and Israel is out of control heading for the far-right side of government and fighting for its survival against Hamas. Plus having troops in over one hundred countries is not cheap.

Michael L. Roeder

The agreement on June 3, 2023, came after months of President Biden and House Speaker McCarthy playing footsie with each other before reaching an agreement just seconds before X Day, the day the government would have defaulted on the national debt. The debt ceiling was raised by four trillion dollars. The President said: "Nobody got everything, but each side got something." That was true but the American people in my view got screwed again because we got a guarantee of more debt over the next two years. We did get a promise of reduced spending and debt reduction, but I doubt many people believe this will happen. The projected budget deficit for this fiscal year (October 1, 2022-September 30, 2023) is 1.5 trillion dollars and will be a lot higher next FY if inflation stays high and we keep giving money away we do not have. The Congressional Budget Office (CBO) has already estimated that the FY 2024 budget deficit will exceed two trillion dollars. This means a tremendous amount of money will be borrowed so that we can pay our federal bills. This will not amount to debt reduction. As a sidebar, I was hoping that the Congress would cancel the seventy-nine dollars a day meal allotment (2,370 dollars a month) it gave its members earlier this year. Do you think this will happen?

(Unless some significant, earth shattering and painful policy changes impacting budgeting, borrowing, and spending are developed and enacted soon, perhaps the next 12 months, the next battle on raising the debt ceiling in 2025 will be a disaster for the world. MLR)

If a Default Occurs

Even though most Americans do not know what happens, and most Americans do not want to know because it really is too painful, our elected officials have a responsibility to know and they do their best to keep us uninformed. This time around the media and the press did an excellent job of informing and educating the public on the debt ceiling drama. There were endless broadcasts and articles on the repercussions for all of us should default occur. There is 100% absolute agreement among politicians, political consultants, think tanks, and the media that a default would cause the following:

- Basic government services would be reduced, many agencies shut down entirely.
- Public health services would be crippled overnight.
- Federal employees would be laid off, many required to work would not get paid immediately or at all.
- An estimated three million civilians would lose their jobs overnight and unemployment compensation payments may not be possible.
- Federal benefits- Medicare, disability payments, civilian federal retirements- would not be paid or only partially paid.
- Personal and business bankruptcies would skyrocket.
- Worldwide trade crashes.
- Stock market impacted investment accounts wiped out.
- Recession
- National debt balloons by 850 billion dollars or more.
- There is a run on the banks.
- Add 130,000 thousand dollars to a 30-year mortgage because of sky high interest rates.
- U.S. credit rating downgraded, raising interest rates on money we borrow in the future.

(In July 2023, Fitch lowered the U. S. credit rating to AA+ from AAA because of this country's increasing debt. This means the

government will borrow money at a higher interest rate in the future. On November 10, 2023, Moody's, a credit rating agency, lowered this country's rating from stable to negative, based on the nation's worsening fiscal position and political polarization. This is all going to come crashing down on all of us at some point. MLR)

This debt ceiling thing has always been and is a political football that costs taxpayers millions of dollars when the Congress and the President go at it every year or so. During the last escapade, several options were discussed to somehow get around the monolithic debt ceiling China Wall. One had the President taking the initiative and proposing federal legislation which would bypass the procedures now driving the debt limit train. This proved to be futile since any legislation would not pass the Republican dominated House, but if it did by some miracle, it would end up in the courts for years. In fact, the few other options went nowhere because all involved parties knew that the courts would be immediately involved. It will be different in the future with a new President and a different Congress.

The one agency that will most definitely be around to monitor the Executive and Legislative branches of the federal government, The Congressional Budget Office, released data recently that shows by 2033, the national debt will increase by 19 trillion dollars, a figure based just on the costs of 13 major bills passed by the Congress and signed by both President Biden and former President Trump and other presidents since 2015. Also, the Trump tax cut cost the Treasury 2 trillion dollars. The CBO has predicted that Social Security and Medicare will be insolvent in ten years unless the Congress imposes dramatic spending cuts or is prepared to raise taxes significantly. The Social Security/Medicare shortfall for FY 2023 will be 561 billion dollars. The interest paid this year on the National Debt (2023) will be seven hundred billion dollars. The interest paid on the FY 2024 debt will exceed one trillion dollars. The recent budget agreement tied into the debt ceiling agreement does little to assuage my fears that this country is heading towards financial

Armageddon and ten years sounds about right if you are an optimist. I was overly optimistic on March 8, 2023, when I saw a New York Times article about a new freshman, a U.S Representative from Oklahoma named Josh Brecheen, a conservative Republican, a rancher, and former state senator. He won on an anti-debt message in November 2022 and arrived in Washington to get right in the thick of the debt ceiling battle. He wants to reduce our debt profile by defunding dictatorial liberal programs and institutions. As I read on, I realized that he was simply another right-wing Republican voted in by MAGA loving right wing Oklahoma voters. Among other things, he wants to reduce foreign aid payments because it fuels an out-of-control federal bureaucracy; he wants to eliminate the Office of Diversity, Equity and Inclusion (DEI) at the Pentagon; he wants to zero out foreign aid to countries that bolster LGBTQ programs; and he wants to slash 3.4 billion dollars from the migration and refugee assistance budget. It sounds like he is heading right for the Freedom Caucus, the far-right wing motorcycle club that goes out of its way to cause trouble in Congress, something we cannot tolerate much longer.

This debt issue is really a budget issue. This year's federal budget is driven by entitlement program costs which take up 66% of the budget. In December 2022, just before the Democrats lost the House, they passed an omnibus bill with 7,200 earmarks. This is not sustainable. This is also an outrage.

Proposals

- Restructure all entitlement programs to include Social Security, Medicare and Medicaid, and federal retirement systems including the military.

- Form a Congressional Work Committee to find an alternative to the debt ceiling process. The political parties must do something to end this frequent requirement which always causes animosity and enormous financial costs.

- Program fraud recovery. I am hopeful that most politicians will consider this as a viable option to reduce budgets in the affected agencies, reduce the number of benefit recipients, and end or at least greatly reduce what has been endemic fraud in many federal entitlement programs for decades. I am convinced that if it is done right, the federal government could recover 3-5 trillion dollars in four years' time.

The Recovery Plan

First, some form of government announcement as to what is going to happen and how it will happen and needs to happen. An appearance on national media during prime time by the President of the United States would set the right tone. The President would explain why this action is necessary for starters. The primary reason is that the country needs to dramatically reduce its spending profile and reduce the amount of fraud occurring in government benefit programs. The strategy to accomplish this national goal in the next four years can leave no program untouched and no source of revenue unclaimed. The President will have to forcefully state that one source of revenue the government will pursue is the illegal receipt of government benefits by our citizens. This includes Social Security and Social Security Disability fraud, Medicare/Medicaid fraud, welfare fraud, small business loan fraud, income tax fraud, low-income tax childcare tax credit programs, and recent massive fraud identified in the 2021-2022 pandemic relief programs with estimated fraud in just those programs in the 250-billion-dollar range (conservative estimate).

The President would announce a timeline which would have a start date with a 3–5-month grace period from the date of his/her speech. He would define the process-who would conduct the effort and how the fraudster could make amends before it is too late. This is the key part of the plan. The President or representative would cover each fraud area and list a 1-800 number to call "Right now", that evening to arrange a meeting with a "Recovery Agent" to pay what is owed which would include a penalty fee of 10%. The penalty fee would go to the agent who would be a contract employee of the federal government. For example, if a person continued to collect a parent's social security benefit for 8 years after the parent died, and that amounted to 96,000 dollars, that person would have to pay 96,000 dollars plus a 10% penalty or a total of 105,600 dollars and forfeit personal Social Security payments for 5 years. Payment would be required upfront, no payment plan. In return, the government would not indict that person. If that person failed to take advantage of the government's generous offer during the grace period and got caught in the ensuing audit of Social Security accounts, that person would be subject to arrest. At that point, it would be too late for a deal. In today's Social Security program, fraud is so rampant, many people may choose to gamble and wait for the hammer to fall. It most likely would not. A real case in point. On July 9, 2023, a New York Times article described how federal investigators had arrested a California man for receiving over 800,000 dollars of his mother's Social Security payments for thirty years after she died in 1990. He also got an annuity payment from her husband's military service. Every month for 33 years, he got a check from Social Security. He agreed to repay 830,000 dollars including his home. He will be sentenced to 30-37 months in federal prison. I do not think this is a rare case.

Each fraud category would have a separate 800 number. The grace period would start from the date of the speech by the president and end when the recovery program starts. Once notified that you are under investigation, it is too late.

While I am not opposed to collection firms experienced in collections, I favor the hiring of contract employees who would receive a commission on what is recovered. I would be comfortable with 10%

plus reimbursement of verified expenses. Individuals acting as contractors would be assigned to the primary agency they are representing. For example, an agent from the Springfield, MA region, working on Social Security fraud would report to someone in the Springfield regional office located in downtown Springfield. That office would also assign the case list for investigation. Agents would work from home and would be responsible for computer systems to conduct investigations. Agents would be required to have a driver's license, a car, be a U. S. citizen, be able to pass a background check, be 100% mobile, and not owe any government any money except for student loans. If they owe a student loan, they cannot be in default. In other words, they go into this clean.

The other major aspect of this idea is how agents would manage business or home visits to verify culpability. The answer would be the presence of military personnel assigned to the regional offices to accompany agents in the field. This idea cannot work without security. Arming agents would never fly currently. Would sending a company of the 101st Airborne Division into Springfield to help work? It could if the President declared a state of "Martial Law," which in fact may be the only way this idea could work. Calling up elements of the U.S. Army Reserve or units of the State National Guard could also work with cooperation of the State governors, but it would be costly.

Why would we need security for these agents? Agents will have to visit homes, bars, businesses, slums, mansions, summer homes, clubs, housing complexes, to look for people who have been dead for years but still getting Social Security, to locate people who have never filed a form 1040, to check on people getting disability from the government who are fully employed, or follow up on people who have claimed hundreds of thousands of dollars in the Payroll Protection Program.

To this day, the federal government does not know how much money is stolen by health care professionals every year. Over the last ten years, the amount has been estimated to exceed a trillion dollars by outside non-government agencies. The amount is well short of reality. I believe the amount is closer to two trillion dollars. There is no more despicable example of corruption in any form than the Medicare Program where the crooks are doctors and other well educated and well-paid health care professionals.

The administrative requirements would be the responsibility of the specific agency tasked with oversight of their part of this massive endeavor.

I acknowledge there are strategic reasons why this idea will not fly. The main reason is that the government will not support it because it is simply too big a project. Citizens will love it and hate it. Conservatives will support it, Progressives will not. If Trump is President, he will support it if he can be convinced that up to four trillion dollars can be returned to the Treasury. Three trillion dollars will meet his requirement. If Biden is President, this thing is dead. Invasion of privacy, violation of the Constitution, impossible to organize and control, rioting in the streets, all these issues will surface overnight.

We put a man on the moon, we created the medicines to control HIV, we got control of the pandemic, we did all this and more so we can structure the administrative ability to recover trillions of dollars stolen from the federal government over the last ten-fifteen years without too much difficulty. It really is a matter of political will. This effort will require the hiring of at least 10,000 contract agents to cover all the agencies and programs in question. A regional approach would be most effective in the execution of the program. The government will put thousands of people to work in what many will consider the most worthwhile and bold plan to bring financial solvency to the U. S. government since the country's founding in the eighteenth century.

The government bureaucrats will figure it all out. I am convinced that the grace period identified by the President will immediately result in hundreds of thousands of phone calls by fraudsters who would be happy to pay up rather than even face the possibility of ending up in jail at some point in the next three years. Imagine living with the idea that at any time in the next 36 months you could be arrested for government fraud. People who commit this type of fraud do not do well in prison. Doctors and other health care fraudsters, for example, will jump at the chance to pay up and avoid a possible lengthy jail sentence and loss of license. They would be happy to sell off that beautiful summer home on Cape Cod to avoid several years at Danbury Federal.

This proposal represents a huge endeavor to be sure, but the recovery amount, which will be in the trillions of dollars, will justify the effort and any startup expenses. As important, it will certainly reset the attitude that exists in this country today that government funds are there for the taking. The Biden administration Progressives made that abundantly clear with its giveaway programs totaling trillions of dollars. Progressives do not care about administrative planning and controls. Since Biden became President in 2021, his progressive friends have proven it time and time again. Examples would be the withdrawal from Afghanistan, a complete disaster, ARPA fraud, a complete disaster; Immigration policy, a complete disaster; economic policy, a complete disaster.

A net reduction in fraud committed against the government will reduce budget expenses and recipient rosters. The long-term savings could represent six trillion dollars over the next decade. Even if I am wrong, one part of the worldwide, nationwide corruption entourage, which I covered in Chapter 5, will have been addressed and this is a good thing. We must get serious finally about reducing government spending. The voters in this country can force a different approach to the budget by using their most powerful tool to force change and that is the individual vote. Otherwise, that will mean 4 more years of hell no matter who gets elected. We would have to look ahead to 2028. In 2028, I will be 84 years old and on my last breath. But my children and grandchildren will not be so it is they I am hoping will figure it out. I am fearful that by 2028, it will be too late. Here is why. Currently, state and local debt totals 6 trillion dollars; consumer debt totals 16.5 trillion dollars; corporate debt totals 10 trillion dollars; federal debt totals 33.6 trillion dollars and the federal government borrows 4 billion dollars every day; commercial property loan delinquencies are at a five year high; credit card delinquencies are heading skyward to new records; and interest rates will remain high for at least two more years. Enough said.

Michael L. Roeder

Chapter 5: Corruption

Webster's Dictionary defines "Corruption" as: "dishonest or illegal behavior committed by especially powerful people (such as government officials or police officers": depravity. B.: inducement to wrong by improper or unlawful means (such as bribery). Transparency International, the well-respected global civil society organization that rates 180 countries on their levels of corruption, last year stated that worldwide corruption is "pervasive and intrusive." Based on the research I have done on this subject, I am convinced that corrupt practices the world over are worsening and destroying, in the extreme, the quality of life in many countries, especially in countries that have the lowest standards of living and leaders that have been and are corrupt to the core to begin with.

At the international level of government, presidents, prime ministers, leaders of legislative bodies, and state-controlled agencies, actively solicit bribes and kickbacks on government contracts, empty national treasuries, sell off natural resources on the black market and steal foreign aid of all kinds. Powerful organized crime groups control markets and trade unions and become so powerful that they run for political office and get elected or choose to operate undercover, if you will, and control high ranking government officials through bribery and coercion.

At the national level of government (state and federal in this country), kickbacks and bribery, gift giving and receiving, officials who go rogue, union officials who bribe elected and appointed officials,

officials who believe they are above the law and commit crimes that impact the public's confidence in government, are out of control. We have that very situation in our federal government "Right now." Power hungry Trump on one side and money hungry Biden is on the other. What kind of society are we where we allow this kind of crap to go on in America? Not to mention George Santos, the U.S. Representative from New York who still thinks lying is perfectly ethical and who has vowed to run for re-election in 2024, even though he faces two recent federal indictments (23 counts) which should land him in federal prison for a few years.

(After two failed attempts to expel him from the U. S. House of Representatives, legislators did finally vote to expel him on December 1, 2023. His final comment on his way out the door: "To hell with this place." MLR)

Then there is the case of the U.S. Senator Bob Menendez (D-NJ), indicted by a Manhattan federal court on bribery and other felony charges on September 21, 2023. His wife Nadine was also charged with similar felony counts. Menendez is the chairman of the Senate Foreign Relations Committee. He has temporarily stepped down from that role. The government case evolves around his relationships with a number of New Jersey based businessmen who lavished Menendez and his wife with lots of cash, around 560,000 thousand dollars, 150,000 thousand dollars in gold bars and a 2019 C-Class Mercedes-Benz valued at 60,000 thousand dollars. The day after his indictment, he announced he would run for re-election in 2024. In 2018, Menendez beat a federal charge of bribery after a hung jury. When all is said and done, it would be truly ironic if he and Trump shared a cell in the same federal prison.

(Postscript: On October 14, 2023, Menendez and his wife were indicted again on a charge of violating the "Foreign Agents Registration Act (FARA)" for failure to register as a foreign agent representing the country of Egypt. He should be expelled from the

U. S. Senate. Give them a fair trial, but if found guilty, no probation, parole, community service, half-way house or ankle bracelets. They should see the inside of a prison for a few years. Members of Congress will take notice, which is a good thing. MLR)

In many countries, entire families or military leaders gain control of government operations and bleed them dry. Just in the last decade, Haiti, El Salvador, Russia, Venezuela, South Africa, Somalia, Yemen, Belarus, and a few more (actually a lot more) countries have been completely taken over by corrupt leaders and hundreds of millions of people are suffering for it. In fact, Transparency International, in its report on corruption in 2022, indicated that governmental corruption is the primary reason for the massive undocumented immigration to our southern border ongoing "Right now" with no sign of letting up.

At the local level of government, consider what you just read because it all happens in city and county government but often on a smaller scale. Still, it is disconcerting when you read about a local resident who pilfered the PTA high school checking account, or the city employee who cleaned out the local municipal union checking account.

A few specific examples will help to prove my position that corruption of all types exists at all levels of government and has made almost impossible our ability to solve or at least manage out of conflict our most pressing problems.

On the world stage, in my view, the most horrific example of corruption is the country of Russia. Twenty years ago, Vladimir Putin became President of this country and immediately and ruthlessly began to dismantle what had been a vastly rich in resources Communist State that controlled everything including all production of goods, many of which nobody in Russia bought. In just a few years he managed to sell off most state run and owned industries to his friends (those who could pay) who are now called "Oligarchs." The plan was simple. Somebody would buy an industry or a resource, let us say timber or oil, at a great price agreed upon by Putin. The buyer would pay a substantial upfront kickback and then an annual commission to Putin. Today, Putin is thought to be worth 210 billion dollars. Not bad when you consider that he earns an annual presidential salary of 187,000 thousand dollars. He owns seventy homes including a 190,000 square foot mansion overlooking the Black Sea that is worth 1.4 billion dollars! He owns seven hundred cars and fifty-five airplanes, believe it or not. That is only the tip of the iceberg on this guy's wealth posture. Many of his Oligarch friends are worth billions as well. Russia is a criminal enterprise pure and simple. Putin is pure evil and a threat to the world. He is currently under indictment by the International Criminal Court (The Hague) for war crimes committed in Ukraine. Specifically, he is charged with masterminding and authorizing the kidnapping of over 100,000 Ukrainian children and sending them to Russia where they are being indoctrinated and then adopted by Russian families.

He has many friends in high places. Alexander Lukashenko is one of them. He is the President of Belarus, a country adjacent to the northeast of Russia. He is pure evil as well, a ruthless and wealthy leader who allowed Putin to stage tactical nuclear weapons at Belarus' border with Ukraine early in 2022. He and Putin have become filthy rich at the expense of citizens of both countries.

In 2008, in this country, Bernie Madoff got 150 years in federal prison for pulling off the largest Ponzi scheme in recorded history. He stiffed thousands of investors and fund managers of private and government investment funds, foreign investors, and managed funds from countries like England and Germany, all taken in by the return on investments they were all receiving every month right on time for years. He had his sons involved. Untold billions of dollars were given to the man to invest. Unfortunately for all these investors, Madoff never invested a dime of that money. Instead, he did what all crooks do, he lived it up in many different countries, had homes in many different countries and owned planes and boats to get to these countries whenever he wanted. Madoff was the best at what he did. The Securities and Exchange Commission (SEC) was on his case off and on for 30 years and never caught him. The great recession of 2008 brought him down because he could not pay his investors when they asked him for their money. In a brief period, he was in jail and his family destroyed by his greed. The fraud has been estimated to be about sixty-four billion dollars. Madoff died in prison on April 14, 2021. His two sons died before he did-one from cancer and one from suicide. His wife lives somewhere in silence.

A New York Post article on December 9, 2023, highlighted the problem of rampant corruption in Latin and Central America. A U.S. State Department official was quoted in the article: "Corruption is a root cause of undocumented immigration to the United States." The article also indicated that widespread corruption among its chief executives undermines public faith. The article made an especially important point that much of the corruption is tied directly to drug trafficking. That would be undeniable if you are considering the histories of Mexico, Columbia, Ecuador, Peru, Honduras, Panama, and El Salvador.

(I do not think I got them all, but I am close. I do realize that the demand for cocaine, "Right now," is at an all-time high in the United States. The reality is bleak I must admit. MLR)

In 2023, Peruvian President Pedro Castillo is in prison for attempting to avoid long standing criminal charges by disbanding the country's Congress. He is facing numerous corruption and graft charges and many years in prison if found guilty. In the past seven years in Peru there have been seven presidents in office. Two former presidents are in prison now on various corruption charges and one has been fighting extradition from the United States for years. All he did was take a 20-million-dollar bribe from a Brazilian construction company in 2016. So did a lot of other government leaders across Latin America. The company said it paid out 807 million dollars to these leaders to get contracts worth billions.

In 2023, the Argentine Supreme Court convicted Vice-President Cristina Kirchner of steering construction contracts worth a billion dollars to friends in return for kickbacks totaling millions of dollars. "Right now," she is awaiting sentence.

In 2019, Brazil President Lula da Silva went to jail on corruption charges. In 2022 he was re-elected president of the country, a genuinely nice reward from the very people he screwed.

In 2020, former President of Honduras, Juan O. Hernandez, was arrested for drug trafficking while in office and was eventually extradited to the United States on April 21, 2022, to stand trial. He is in jail awaiting his trial which is scheduled for September 2023. His brother was recently sentenced to life in prison for drug trafficking.

Since February 2022, Ukraine has been defending itself against an invasion of its sovereign land by Russia and is receiving massive amounts of cash and military aid from many NATO member countries, including over one hundred billion dollars in foreign and military aid from the United States. The problem was, before Volodymyr Zelensky was elected President of Ukraine in 2019 on an anti-corruption ticket, the country was notoriously corrupt at every level of government. The country was under the control of Putin before and after the collapse of Communism in Eastern Europe. When Ukraine declared its independence and elections were held, every president elected proceeded to rob the country blind. There were citizen revolts one after the other. Finally in 2019, Zelensky, a well-known and popular comedian-actor, won the presidency. One of his first acts was to establish a federal anti-corruption unit, the best thing he could have done based on what is happening in the country "Right now."

Since Zelensky has come to power, super serious incidents of corruption have occurred. This has caused some NATO members and some extreme right Republicans in the U.S. Congress to raise doubts about future commitments. On January 24, 2023, Zelensky fired a deputy minister for taking a 406,000-dollar bribe in an equipment purchasing scandal. In May 2023, another deputy minister was arrested for taking kickbacks on awards of food purchasing contracts for Ukraine military. In July 2023, all fifteen regional military recruit supervisors in the country were fired by Zelensky for taking bribes from civilians looking to evade the military draft. On May 18, 2023, the Chief of Ukraine's Supreme Court was arrested with two other judges for taking a 1.8-million-dollar bribe to squash corruption charges against a Ukraine Oligarch who had escaped to France and was fighting extradition. The judge was also caught red-handed accepting a bribe from a lawyer in another case. The judge now sits in prison awaiting trial. It is noteworthy that the anti-corruption unit was involved in every case. It is also noteworthy that the unit now has ongoing over two hundred active corruption cases.

(God help us if Zelensky gets caught up in any corruption activities. His formation of the anti-corruption unit was an example of good planning for his country and himself. MLR)

In 2022, Transparency International rated South Sudan, separated from Sudan in Southern Africa ten years ago, the most corrupt country out of the 180 countries it rates annually. The country's current civil war has devastated it. Over 400,000 citizens have died and untold billions of dollars have gone missing in a very oil rich nation. Starvation is rampant. Food aid ends up on the black market. All this is happening, and the country's leadership has no idea where the aid money and the oil money went. Offshore banks might be one place to look. The Transparency Int. score for Sudan in 2022 was thirteen out of one hundred points. The

United States gave this country 926 million dollars in foreign aid in 2022. How is this possible? What are we thinking?

(I will be writing about our foreign aid program and its relationship to the Transparency International process later in this chapter. MLR)

On March 10, 2023, the New York Post published an article on Roger Ng, the former head of Foreign Banking in Malaysia, for the investment bank Goldman Sachs. NG got a ten-year prison sentence for paying the very top leaders of the government, starting with Prime Minister Najib Razak, who got twelve years in prison for accepting ten million dollars in bribes from NG. With NG leading the way, billions of dollars were looted from the country's IMDB Sovereign Wealth Fund. The country barely survived the looting and is still recovering.

In this country, there is no dearth of corruption stories to tell. Corruption in government, industry, finance and banking, frauds of all types, with a good number designed to prey on our elderly population, exists everywhere and it is taking a terrible toll on the American psyche and pocketbook.

In 2023, several major crypto-currency fraud schemes have become known. The biggest by far was the FTX/Alameda fiasco, engineered by a 31-year-old boy named Sam Bankman-Fried. He and one Caroline Ellison, twenty-eight and one Gary Wang, 29, took a break from their play-dough games and conspired to steal, misappropriate, squander, whatever term you want, billions of investor dollars to lead the high life and impress. They engaged in criminal activity from the start in 2019 and never got caught until late 2022. Ellison and Wang have already pleaded guilty and will be sentenced after they testify against Fried in federal court, all in the hope of getting leniency for themselves from the judge. At some point, Fried will take a plea and do his thirty years in prison unless he is out of his mind. FTX was the "helter-skelter" of finance. Anything was a go. Recordkeeping was for the common man.

The two companies handled billions of invested dollars and hardly kept any records. Wang, who was the FTX chief technical officer, was able to take six million dollars of company funds for his personal use and never pay it back. Nishad Singh, also arrested, was the FTX director of engineering. He got a company loan for 543 million dollars and never paid a dime back. This was all revealed when FTX filed for bankruptcy in November 2022. At some point, I would hope that the SEC will step in and regulate this crypto currency debacle big time. "Right now," there are at least three other crypto frauds in the U.S. federal courts amounting to more billons of pilfered investor dollars.

(Much to my surprise, Sam went to trial in October 2023 in Manhattan Federal Court and was found guilty of 6 of 7 fraud counts on November 2, 2023. He had been in jail on bail revocation several weeks before. He is scheduled for sentencing on March 28, 2024. He faces 110 years in a federal prison. The jury deliberated for four hours. MLR)

In a March 14, 2023, New York Post article on COVID-19 related fraud, ten people were charged with stealing 250 million dollars from a federal COVID-19 aid program that fed low-income children during the pandemic. Charges included conspiracy, wire fraud, money laundering and bribery. The Federal Child Nutrition Program was ripped off in 2021-2022. Since the initial indictments, an additional thirty-seven people have been arrested. The article covered an early 2023 analysis by the Associated Press (AP) on COVID-19 disbursements from the aid spending programs that were passed by the Congress and signed off by two presidents to blunt the impacts of the pandemic. The report stated that 4.2 trillion dollars have been distributed since the end of 2020. The AP analysis shows that some 280 billion dollars has been stolen, 123 billion dollars has been wasted and another one hundred billion dollars is being investigated. "Right now," 3,195 people have been arrested for fraud and thousands of cases ("Right now" that number is 163,000) are under investigation. The money went to overseas organized crime gangs, prisoners, drug gangs, foreign racketeers, ordinary U.S. citizens seizing on an opportunity and citizens living in Nigeria.

On June 20, 2023, the Springfield Republican, a daily newspaper published in Springfield, MA, did an editorial that deserved a national spotlight for the "unspeakable crimes that were committed" at Harvard Medical School's Anatomical Gifts Program. Cedric Lodge, a long-term employee at the school, was allowing people to come to the mortuary at the school and purchase body parts from cadavers donated to the school for research. One person paid the employee $600 dollars for two faces from cadavers. The buyer wanted to have the faces tanned into leather. That also happened back in Germany during WW II and a lot of people got hanged for their involvement in that practice. It gets worse and more perverse. Parts of 350-400 cadavers might have been sold over the years. They included heads, brains, skin, bones, and organs. It was all done for money and lots of it. Forget probation, fines, community service, restitution, ankle bracelets, a halfway house program or a suspended sentence. Several employees were involved. This case cries out for serious jail time for anyone who even brushed up against this demented behavior.

On April 27, 2023, the New York Times did an article on the "Build the Wall" fraud that allowed four individuals to raise twenty-five million dollars to build the wall at our southern border, the very wall that Donald Trump wanted to build while he was President of the United States. In 2019, Brain Kolfage, a triple amputee Air Force veteran injured in Iraq, formed a non-profit group "Build the Wall" to construct the border barrier Trump had promised. There were three co-founders: Tim Shea from Colorado, Andrew Badolato, a financier and Stephen K. Bannon, a former advisor to you guessed it, Donald Trump. Their mantra was: "All money raised would go towards the wall." This turned out to be complete bullshit.

In 2020, the federal government accused these four individuals of receiving hundreds of thousands of dollars for personal expenses such as boat payments. Badolato and Kolfage pled guilty to wire fraud conspiracy in 2022. In the fall of 2022, Shea was convicted of wire fraud and laundering money. Bannon also faced federal criminal charges but was pardoned by Trump. However, he still faces state charges in New York state courts. Trump cannot touch that. On Wednesday, April 26, 2023, Badolato got 36 months and Kolfage got 51 months in federal prison. The non-profit raised more than twenty-five million dollars. Kolfage was actually paid an initial one hundred thousand dollars and then twenty thousand dollars a month after that. One million dollars was funneled from the non-profit to another non-profit group formed by Bannon called "Citizens of the American Public," which channeled money to Bannon and Kolfage. Hundreds of thousands went to Shea through a company called "Ranch Property Marketing and Management." Money also went to Badolato through the "White Knights and Vulture Company." Bannon is free pending state trial and raising hell on his immensely popular Podcast show based in Washington, DC, just a few blocks from the U.S. Capitol.

On March 15, 2023, a New York Post article "Black Lives Matter in Red for 8 million", described how the BLM Global Network Foundation ended 2022 in the red 8.5 million dollars. The foundation had raised 8.5 million dollars but managed to spend seventeen million dollars with most of the money going to relatives of the former co-founder of Black Lives Matter (BLM) Patrisso Cullors. Approximately 1.69 million dollars went to a company owned by then BLM President, Shalomyah Bowers, for management and consulting services. BLM board member Danielle Edwards owned a firm that was paid 1 million + dollars for consulting services. Cullors' brother, Paul, BLM's only paid employee, received 140 thousand dollars in compensation but his security firm, Black Ties LLC, was paid 756 thousand dollars for security services. Ms. Cullors lost her position as president of BLM when it was discovered she had used BLM funds to purchase several high-priced California homes she and her relatives live in to this day. Her home cost six million dollars. Not bad if you get away with it, which looks like they have "Right now."

On the local, community level across the country, there are thousands of cases involving criminal fraud related activities-municipal fraud, bribery, kickbacks and the like. Local fraud also entails civic checking accounts being emptied by the volunteer treasurer. And municipal employees are caught stealing union funds they manage. This happened recently in Westfield, MA, my hometown, where a municipal employee was charged with stealing seven thousand dollars from a union checking account he had sole control over. A career ender and a 97-thousand-dollar salary out the window. It also happened recently in Springfield, MA where three YMCA employees allegedly stole 28, 900 dollars from a state funded program for domestic violence victims. They are all awaiting trial in state court. On May 5, 2023, a former president of the Massachusetts State Police troopers Union got 2.5 years in a federal prison for accepting kickbacks from a lobbyist and for misuse of a union debit card. The lobbyist got two years for accepting a 20-thousand-dollar bribe. The thinking is "I will not get caught. That guy over there will but I will not." This type of behavior will go on forever but there is simply too much of it happening "Right now." Many of the people (cases) I wrote about in this, and other chapters did get prison time, which I think is appropriate. The question is, is the amount of time given sufficient to persuade people watching not to commit that same type of crime? The answer is NO. This means that the problem of corruption will never be managed properly, especially today because in many communities, and in progressive blue communities in particular, the view is not to prosecute many crimes. I saw it in the Springfield District Court, I saw it in the Westfield District Court. Many of the charges in these courts are profoundly serious. They involve the sale of drugs, the scourge of all communities, domestic violence, assaults on the elderly, gang violence, property damage, car vandalism (addicts looking for anything they can sell) and car theft. In Westfield in particular, 90% of all defendants are released on low or no bond with pre-trial conditions, a typical behavior in the progressive courts in a progressive state which Massachusetts is. In the Westfield court, 98% of all dispositions end up with no jail time.

U.S. Foreign Aid Program

Why is this country's foreign aid program in a chapter focusing on corruption?

The answer I believe is simple. It does not come in a few lines of explanation, however. This book is attempting to identify major problem areas impacting this country's well-being and future, which is linked to economic viability and federal and state budgets that are realistic and doable. Current spending levels at the federal level and in many states threaten our futures. Debt loads are sky high. California has a debt of 520 billion dollars; New York, 368 billion dollars; Texas, 324 billion dollars, Florida, 131 billion dollars; Illinois, 159 billion dollars. If government is bankrupt then society is doomed, and I happen to think that is where we are headed.

In Fiscal Year (FY) 2022, the U.S. foreign aid budget was thirty-eight billion dollars. In FY 2024, the proposed foreign aid budget is 63.1 billion dollars. The Corruption Perception Index (CPI) published by Transparency International (TI), rates 180 countries on their perceived level of corruption based on a review of thirteen different variables reported by different international organizations like the World Bank. Zero points indicate a country is very corrupt; one hundred points indicates the opposite. The global average for FY 2022 is forty-three. Seventy percent (126) of the 180 countries scored below 50. The twenty-four countries that made the list for being the most corrupt also made this book. They are listed here with their CPI score, their ranking based on that score and the amount of foreign aid they received from the United States in FY 2022:

Country	CPI Score	Ranking	Foreign Aid Received
Somalia	12	1	$1.13 Billion
South Sudan	13	2	$820 Million
Syria	13	2	$876 Million
Congo	13	2	$897 Million
Venezuela	14	3	$208 Million
Yemen	16	4	$1 Billion
Libya	17	5	$51 Million
Burundi	17	5	$112 Million
Haiti	17	5	$309 Million
Chad	19	6	$108 Million
Nicaragua	19	6	$23 Million
Turkmenistan	19	6	$4 Million
Dem Rep Congo	20	7	$841 Million
Sudan	22	8	$488 Million
Zimbabwe	23	9	$399 Million
Honduras	23	9	$200 Million
Iraq	23	9	$512 Million
Myanmar	23	9	$208 Million
Guatemala	24	10	$245 Million
Nigeria	24	10	$1.1 Billion
Afghanistan	24	10	$4 Billion
Central Africa	24	10	$196 Million
Lebanon	24	10	$463 Million
Bangladesh	25	11	$373 Million
			$14.5 Billion

The United States has a current and growing national debt of 33.5 trillion dollars (as of September 19, 2023) and we can still find the time to give away 14 + billion dollars to twenty-four of the most corrupt countries on the face of this earth. This is only the tip of the iceberg. In

FY 2022, we gave out billions more to countries that were only a little less corrupt and to countries that hardly needed our money.

Analysis

Somalia: In 2022, this laid waste country scored a twelve on the Corruption Perception Index (CPI) issued by Transparency International. Corruption at all levels of government and society has prevented any foreign aid or bank aid from having any impact on improving the country. Over the years drought and military conflict have wreaked havoc. A terrorist group, Al-Shabaab, has conducted Jihadi military and political operations against the new government. Since mid-2022 government backed uprisings against this group have been ineffective. Half the population faces acute food insecurity, five hundred thousand children suffer severe malnutrition, ¾ of the country's three million livestock have died. Bad governance, stalled elections, clan rivalries, Al-Shabaab urban terror, massive corruption and a black market that gobbles up about everything all adds up to ongoing death and destruction. This country has been in a collapsed state since 1991. Non-Government Agencies (NGOs) no longer bring aid because it disappears into the wind. The U. S. Government has known this for years and yet our aid keeps flowing in. Where it goes no one in the Somali Government (what there is of it) knows. In 2022, this country received 1.1 billion dollars in U. S. foreign aid. A complete disaster!

South Sudan: With a CPI score of 13, this country, separated from Sudan twelve years ago, has been mired in civil conflict, drought, starvation, and recent flooding. It currently has the largest refugee crisis in Africa, the third largest in the world. The country is mired so deep in corruption activities, there are experts who believe the country is doomed. The country operates as a kleptocracy. Clan's fight each other for power and grab as much money as they can along the way. A U.N. Auditor General's report issued in 2012 estimated that more than four billion dollars in government funds have been stolen since 2005 when the country was granted self-rule. The ruling elite and their families are wealthy beyond imagination while a large segment of the population is food insecure and jobless. In FY 2022, U.S. foreign aid totaled 820 million dollars. The year before it was over a billion dollars. The country is rich in oil reserves.

Haiti: Haiti has a well-deserved reputation as a country riddled with one disaster after another, no matter what the event, a presidential assassination, a hurricane, an earthquake, gang violence, corrupt cops, and an elite kleptocracy that, over the years, must be considered one of the longest and deepest ever to exist on this planet. Going all the way back to the Duvalier days, many decades ago the country was known for violence against its own people and corruption so deep it is still at the forefront of the everyday tragedy we see in that country today. It is the poorest country in the Western Hemisphere, despite billions of dollars thrown at it by the U.S. and international money lenders like the International Monetary Fund (IMF). From 1995-2003, the U.S. gave Haiti 850 million dollars; from 2004-2006, over six hundred million dollars; in 2007, 198 million dollars; in FY 2022, 309 million dollars. Haitians are migrating to the United States in record numbers "Right now."

Venezuela: This is one country that deserves nothing from anybody. With A CPI of 14, the country is tightly controlled by the Maduro family which has created a Kleptocracy that has destroyed the economy, wiped out millions of jobs, brought inflation to record levels, and has driven millions out of the country. That includes two million people to Columbia and close to two hundred thousand Venezuelans arriving in the U.S. in the last two years and more arriving every day. Ask Mayor Adams of New York city-he can give you the latest numbers. President Nicholas Maduro runs a criminal enterprise called Venezuela and keeps control through a ruthless mafia- like organization. The country has one of the highest murder rates in the world. As far back as 2019, the U. S.

no longer recognized Maduro as president. Embassy operations were suspended. On March 26, 2020, Maduro and many others were indicted on drug trafficking charges in a Florida federal court. Billions of dollars were involved. That same year Florida prosecutors seized 450 million dollars in a Florida barn. The money had been put there by high-ranking officials in the Maduro administration. Venezuela is an oil rich state with oil reserves worth trillions. It is the largest oil reserve in the world. The people do not benefit from it. This is what takes my breath away. In March of 2023, the U. S. pledged 171 million dollars in humanitarian assistance and development funding to this country. In September 2022, the U. S. provided 376 million dollars in humanitarian aid. Foreign aid in 2022 amounted to 209 million dollars. As a taxpayer, this kind of financial incompetence by our elected and appointed officials who are entrusted with the execution of our aid programs, is a national travesty and tragedy.

Afghanistan: You would think that after twenty years in that country and after spending over a trillion dollars during that time on development of a democratic government/society that valued women and gave everyone a chance at success, in a country so corrupt, that we would say today, we did the best we could and moved on. The CPI rating of thirteen is a generous rating. It really should be zero. If you look at this country's allocations of foreign aid for FY 2022, Afghanistan was scheduled to get four billion dollars. But this country left Afghanistan in August of 2021, the absolute disaster that it was, so I was shocked to see that huge amount of money. I researched further and found another government document that listed FY 2022 foreign aid at 1.3 million dollars. I could not understand that amount either. The Taliban came into power in 2021 and erased overnight all the progress made since 2002. We should not be surprised. Bribery, graft at all levels of government, deep nepotism, illegal land transfers, police corruption, clan conflicts, ghost Army payrolls, a complete disaster since the U.S. arrived in 2002. The most classic example of how bad this was occurred in 2010 when the Kabul National Bank revealed that over one billion dollars had been looted from the bank and it was bankrupt. U.S. investigations revealed that most of the money had been diverted by members of President Hamid Karzai's inner circle. A few people got arrested but Karzai escaped unharmed. Karzai then demanded that the U. S. fork over a billion dollars so the bank could pay its bills. We did not do that, but it did nothing to reduce losses. The experts on Afghanistan estimate that between 20-30 % of the trillion dollars we spent in that country was looted by successive Afghan administrations. At 20%, that would amount to two hundred billion dollars.

Yemen: Is the poorest country in the Middle East. Wikipedia describes the country as crippled by incessant war and institutionalized corruption which has been entrenched for decades. From 1990-2012 President Ali Saleh and his family took over the government and military. They became wealthy beyond words because of their greed and dishonesty. It is estimated that during his reign, sixty billion dollars was looted from the banks, government agencies, military aid, foreign aid, nothing was scared. In 2018, 2 billion dollars in USAID aid placed in Yemen's Central Bank was looted. President Abed Hadi was the main suspect but nothing much happened. Nothing much ever happens to these crooks. The current war in Yemen started in 2014. "Right now," Yemen deaths total 233, 000 and the general population is food insecure. Iran and Saudi Arabia are involved. There are two governments running the country, one in Sana'a and one in Aden, both recognized as corrupt. U.S. foreign aid to Yemen in 2022, 1 billion dollars! And still, the Houthis in Yemen send missiles to the Red Sea every day.

In all these countries, corruption plays a significant role in the functioning of government and society. The ruling elites, universally, could care less about the people they are supposed to be taking care of. Instead, they steal everything they can until there is nothing left. For me, the rhetorical question is: "Should we be giving these corrupt leaders our money when our own government is deeply in debt and spends more money than it takes in on a daily basis?" I know the answer and the answer is NO!! This cannot go on much longer. We came close to disaster in June 2023 when the debt ceiling almost did not make it. Every administration since Harry Truman has been giving away our hard-earned money to maintain influence in world affairs but I am not sure it is working that well today. The FY 2024 foreign aid budget has been published and "Right now" it is projected at sixty-three billion dollars, up from thirty-four billion dollars in 2023. That huge increase, which will be passed by Congress, exists because of the war in Ukraine and that is another story altogether. I wonder aloud what the Hamas invasion of Israel on October 7, 2023, will have on that sixty-three billion dollars and what will happen to our support of Ukraine at the same time. Something will have to give.

Ukraine: The question that is developing "Right now" is how much support can be given to this country in the long term? There are rumblings in the U. S. Congress from the hard right mostly, that monetary support must have an end date because of the cost involved. The U. S. has given 100 billion+ dollars in cash and military weaponry to Ukraine since the invasion in February 2022. The corruption in Ukraine that I alluded to in this book is another factor unfortunately, that some world leaders are looking at. It seems to me that our continued support of Ukraine in this struggle for survival means that we will have no choice but to redirect most foreign aid allocations from other countries to Ukraine. If Trump is elected, Ukraine is doomed at least in terms of our continuing monetary and military aid support. If Biden is elected, we will continue to spend billions of dollars no matter for how long. Ukraine has a CPI of 32 because President Zelensky has made significant inroads against corruption in that country, despite the continuing arrests of government officials in the Executive and Judicial branches of government.

(I just hope Zelensky stays clean. If he does not, that could be the straw that breaks the camel's back. I cannot imagine Zelensky is on the take in any shape or manner. MLR)

Israel: One thing for me is certain. Never again can we permit any onslaught against the country of Israel and its people. In 1948, the Arab countries attacked Israel with the intent of destroying its infrastructure and driving its people into the sea. That, after years of slaughter in Europe during WW II. In FY 2022, Israel was scheduled to receive three billion dollars in foreign aid from the U. S. Its CPI score was sixty-three points, way above the average. The country has had a few scandals; it does use its aid wisely. It should be no surprise to anyone that this country has one of the best equipped and best trained armed forces in the world. I went to military school with Israeli officers back in the nineties. They were on a survival mission then and nothing has changed in that regard. Having said that, the current situation in the country may force the United States to reduce its foreign aid for several key reasons. First, the country is wealthy, people are prosperous. Second, the recent government coalition formed by newly elected Prime Minister Benjamin Netanyahu, under indictment on several corruption cases since 2019 (prosecution currently suspended after he was elected prime minister). The coalition is made up of ultra conservatives and hard right zealots who, with Netanyahu, want to dramatically reduce the power of the country's Supreme Court. This has caused the people of Israel to riot daily in opposition to this maneuver. They want the court to stay exactly as it is "Right now." Third, the war in Ukraine may cause major disruptions in foreign aid disbursements in FY 2024. Fourth, many in the U.S. Congress, both Democrats and Republicans, believe the several billion dollars a year in foreign aid payments to a wealthy country must end.

(The invasion of Israel by the terrorist organization, Hamas, with its slaughter of innocent men, women, and children, killing over a thousand Israelis the first day, the world order is facing dramatic change. If Israel invades Gaza, it will do so until the Hamas

organization is destroyed. If Hezbollah invades northern Israel, Israel has the manpower to defend itself but will need military resupply for an extended period, at great cost to the United States. If Iran gets publicly involved it will not be to support Israel. Already, Israeli airstrikes have caused great death and destruction in Gaza and Hamas knew this would happen. They wanted this to happen. So, we have Europe on edge and now we have the Middle East on edge as well. This would be the right time for China to invade Taiwan. MLR)

Proposals

- The Security and Exchange Commission (AEC) and the Congress must waste no time in regulating the crypto-currency industry. The hundreds of billions of dollars that have been lost and the lives that have been ruined by greed deserve justice and impact legislation would simply be one approach to solving this problem.

- Suspend the federal foreign aid program for three years, except for Ukraine and now Israel, to conduct a top to bottom review of the operation. The Transparency International Corruption Perception Index (CPI) should be considered as a barometer for future distribution of funds and any country getting less than a score of 50 would receive no funding. Giving U.S. taxpayer money to corrupt countries/leaders is stupid. Nikki Haley would agree 100%.

- Eliminate plea bargaining in all federal fraud related cases. Set maximum bonds that require 100% cash payments. No bondsman. Increase prison sentences.

- With such rampant, out of control fraud existing in federal benefit programs, establish strict oversight in the future. Allocate more personnel to manage and execute program requirements and mandates set by law. Especially the audit responsibility.

Michael L. Roeder

Chapter 6: Climate Change

For every person out there, who is predicting a world environmental collapse if we do not get off our collective asses and work toward the development of effective climate change policies and programs, there is a person out there who is predicting that the present climate related disasters are nothing more than a cyclical phenomenon that will pass as it always has. It is the believers (me) up against the non-believers (you?). Just like in politics.

("Right now," the extremists on the left are in control and the extremists on the right want control back. What do the moderates in our society think should happen in the next decade to blunt climate disaster? This is a rhetorical question; the answer is the elimination of fossil fuels in our daily lives. Unfortunately, it is not going to happen, and I will make a compelling argument for that position much to my personal chagrin. MLR)

The summer climate events of 2023-the hurricanes, micro-bursts, fires, floods, torrential downpours, droughts, pollution, record high tides, dried up rivers- tell me that something serious regarding climate is taking place all over the world, that it is real and that something has to be done on a global scale to avoid the Apocalypse. Thankfully, concern about the world's climate has been a topic for discussion, planning and allocation of resources for years but only recently has it become a serious point of emphasis for media powerhouses, powerful NGOs, and world leaders from rich and poor countries alike. You certainly can judge for yourself how much progress has been made on fossil fuel issues, renewable energy, coal production issues, carbon reduction, and water conservation, based on the articles that follow.

On September 9, 2023, The New York Times published an article entitled: "Climate Report Card." In 2015, an agreement called the "Paris Treaty Agreement" was signed by most world leaders who agreed to submit their environmental plans to fight climate change. The "Global Stockade" countries of 2015 agreed to share committee reports and findings for the first time in 2023. "Right now," the good news is that since 2015, the worst-case climate scenarios predicted in the early 2000's are less likely today. (Really?) The rise in global greenhouse gases has notably slowed. (Really?) The unwelcome news is that there is disagreement on who should be doing more in the long term, the United States, China, India, the European Union? Developing nations cannot move quickly because they lack funding, so they want more money from the industrialized countries. The problem with this approach is that many of these developing countries are historically corrupt and hopelessly in debt as well and most industrialized countries are hopelessly in debt period. The United States would be a perfect example of a country hopelessly in debt.

The United Nations is involved with COP 28, an initiative to foster communication and cooperation among the industrialized and developing countries concerning climate control. There are dozens of international and national organizations out there as well, all trying to move towards the goal for the eventual score and victory. In fact, these environmental organizations are so plentiful and have so much advice to give, the information overload is a lot to manage and distribute. I am not sure the key players are listening.

(Considering recent climate driven events everywhere, we must give this our best shot because so much is at stake. Under the Paris Agreement wealthy emitters like the United States, China, and the European Union, agreed to provide developing countries one

hundred billion dollars annually, beginning in 2020. In 2020, just three years ago, eighty-three billion dollars was provided. There is not much to show for it, and would anyone be surprised? Giving millions, billions of dollars to crooked leaders with a penchant for stealing money, I am not confident that part of the plan will go forward much even in the short term and if it does not, how can the plan succeed? Worse, billions won't do the trick even if no money ended up in Swiss bank accounts. The developing countries will demand trillions of assistance dollars to shift from fossil fuels and engage in adaptation projects like building a sea wall. Industrialized countries will have to spend trillions of dollars as well in the next decade to meet their own climate goals. Where does all this money come from? MLR)

I think a global approach can work if the emphasis at that level is on dissemination of information and oversight, from the United Nations, although I do not have a lot of confidence in that organization based on its performance on the world stage the last 25 years. A concerted world effort is one thing, a regional effort involving just several countries with regional control of assets is another. There is a lot going on now with our climate. The summer of 2023 was an environmental disaster-bad weather, bad everything everywhere. The critical issue is the approach, the strategies, leadership, funding, and participation of financial and business corporations (because government cannot do this alone.)

Speaking of the United Nations, on Monday, September 19, 2023, a conference on climate was held at the United Nations in New York. The purpose of the conference was to review the "Sustainable Development Goals (SDG) developed by the UN way back in 2016. The idea then was to have the involved countries develop climate targets. The goal was to reach these targets by 2030. Instead of selecting the top 5 or 6, the UN organizers adopted 169 targets. "Right now," everyone in the climate change business knows that not one of the targets was met. A lot of money was wasted. I would imagine that the conference attendees will hopefully produce fewer targets and be successful at hitting them. U.N. Secretary General Antonio Guterres wants member countries to contribute five hundred billion dollars each year for the rest of the decade as a stimulus package for climate projects selected at the conference. That is 3.5 trillion dollars over the next 7 years! It will not happen. In 2023 the U. S. Government will tentatively distribute sixty-one billion dollars of humanitarian aid to the world. American philanthropists and charities will spend thirty billion dollars. President Biden's Inflation Reduction Act, passed in 2022, provides up to 1.2 trillion dollars in tax breaks, credits, and cash incentives for climate change initiatives. That is a trillion dollars that will be lost to the U.S. Treasury over time. The UN will expect the U.S.to pony up for the world and that will be impossible. I have no idea when this country is going to suffer the inevitable financial collapse, but it is coming because this administration is financially clueless.

I have chosen to write about several climate disasters that occurred the summer of 2023 and then contrast that with several of the major initiatives being executed around the world to combat climate change.

- In the state of Vermont, specifically the capital city of Montpelier, and more specifically the downtown section of that city, so much rain fell so quickly that the entire downtown was flooded out causing a degree of damage never seen in that area before. Streets, roads, bridges, homes, and businesses were destroyed.

- In Phoenix Arizona, the population suffered through fifteen straight days of 110-degree weather, a record for a city that is used to high temperatures.

- Wildfire smoke from Canada (British Columbia) impacted much of the United States. It reached my hometown of Westfield, MA more than once. I could see the haze and smell it. Thirty-eight million acres of forest burned in that country during the summer. These fires released 1.5 billion tons of carbon dioxide into the atmosphere.

- Eight inches of rain fell on West Point, NY in a few hours. It is considered a once in a thousand-year event.

- In the Arctic Circle, native Inuit's experienced temperatures consistently above 90 degrees.

- Snowpacks everywhere are disappearing at record rates.

- Heavy rains in Sweskin, Japan washed away homes, hospitals, businesses, roads and cut off power and water to hundreds of homes. It was the heaviest rain ever experienced in that region.

- In Spain, temperatures reached 109 degrees, drying up aquifers, lakes, and rivers. The country witnessed the hottest temperatures in its recorded history.

- In Uruguay, a three-year drought has reduced the country's largest reservoir, the Paso Severio, which supplies water to half of the country's 3.4 million people, to 15% capacity. Montevideo, the Capitol, has been on strict water rationing for over a year.

- Wildfires on the Greek Island of Rhodes have caused many deaths and massive destruction. The Lahaina, Hawaii fire killed one hundred people. It was the deadliest U.S. fire in one hundred years.

- The largest river in Central Iran has run completely dry and temperatures in Southern Iran have reached 152 degrees.

- The earth's oceans are the hottest ever recorded in modern history. In the Florida Keys, one oceanic reading in the summer of 2023 hit 101.1 degrees, a world record.

- Commercial fishermen off Cape Cod, MA are reporting that cod have disappeared from waters off that coast. Experts contend that these fish have moved north to colder waters, but what the cod do not know is that North Atlantic waters are experiencing record warm readings.

- July 6, 2023, was the hottest day on the earth in the past forty-four years.

There is more.

The Colorado River is drying up. "Right now," at the Glen Canyon Dam and Lake Powell above the dam, tons of sand and mud have been deposited into that lake every day unnoticed. The dam became operational in 1963, so this deposit scenario has been going on for the past sixty years. Because of the great overuse of the Colorado River and the impact of climate change, the lake is now at 23% of its capacity. The silt has now been exposed and has formed into giant mud blobs moving towards the dam at the rate of one hundred feet a day. These blobs pose a serious threat to the region's water supply, potentially clogging up the drainpipes under the dam and even threatening the integrity of the dam, which is a major source of electrical power for the region. The other dam on that river, Hoover Dam, is at 28% capacity and has its own set of problems.

Three states depend on the Colorado River-Arizona, California, and Nevada- and all three want their fair share. The problem "Right now" is how to determine a fair share. The U. S. Department of the Interior, working with the U. S. Bureau of Reclamation, has decided the best solution would be an agreement worked out by the three states and that is what is developing now. If there is no states' agreement, then the federal government will step in and decide for them based on the principle of "Senior Water Rights" which will mean many years of litigation in federal court. There are four other states below the Hoover Dam that draws water directly from the Colorado River. They are also involved in this ongoing cluster. It is well to remember that this Southwest region of the country has been under drought conditions for the last ten years. In the summer of 2022, Lake Meade dropped to its lowest level.

What We Are Doing

Europe has consistently missed carbon emissions goals and has failed to invest in the solution. (Europe is warming quicker than anyplace else in the world.) It is not surprising that many in Europe, especially in Italy, are suffering from "Eco-anxiety," a not yet clinically recognized condition which focuses on people feeling a sense of gloom and doom about the climate disasters plaguing the world and the feeling that it will only get worse.

When Biden became President in 2021, the very first thing he did officially was cancel the XL Pipeline Project to show Trump who was now in charge. Actually, the progressives and the environment people praised the act as a great strategic step in fighting climate change. There was a lot of talk then about renewable energy projects, alternative energy source development, and the like. Biden let the world know that fossil fuels were on the way out. A funny thing happened on the way to the 2024 election. Late in the summer of 2023, this same Biden approved the Willow Project, an 8 billion dollar oil production operation in the North Slope of the state of Alaska inside the National Petroleum Reserve, a 23 million acre area 200 miles north of the Arctic Circle, a project that would produce 600 million barrels of crude oil over a thirty year span. It would release 280 million tons of carbon emissions into the atmosphere, the equivalent of adding two million cars to our highways annually. Conoco Oil was happy and so will the 2,500 individuals who will be hired to work the project at an average annual salary of 100,000 dollars. Biden will be happy as the project will feed seventeen billion dollars into the U.S. Treasury.

The progressives went bullshit over this announcement. Two weeks later, Biden cancelled all remaining approved drilling contracts in that reserve area, contracts that had been signed off by Congress and signed by Biden previously. This is the type of thing he does which drives everyone crazy, friend and foe alike. Under Trump, the XL project would have remained a go, the Willow Project would have been a go and the seven approved contracts cancelled by Biden would have been a go just for starters. Progressive Democrats would have been angry at that. Republicans thought that Biden shot himself in the foot again. Just like he did when he signed off on withdrawal from Afghanistan without telling anybody.

In August of 2022, Biden signed the 248-billion-dollar Chips and Science Act. This legislation is devoted to the development of semi-conductor manufacturing in the United Sates and the advancement of clean energy projects. Fifty percent of the states have passed laws mandating utilities increase the use of renewable energy to power their plants. This legislation is loaded with tax credits and subsidies to achieve the legislative goals. Most people thought this legislation was a good thing. It is a good thing despite the cost. Republicans thought it was too much money because the country now carries a growing national debt of over thirty-three trillion dollars.

That same year, he signed off on The Inflation Reduction Act, a trillion dollar+ piece of legislation that was really a climate change initiative that projected to reduce greenhouse gases 42% by 2030. The legislation is enormous in scope. Billions of dollars to communities that suffered past environmental harm, i.e., a wind farm for a Sioux tribal community, a green technology company in West Virginia which has mostly lost its coal industry. The goal of the legislation is to create a coalition of the willing to transform the way energy is produced and consumed. This is a fantastic opportunity for communities to join to solve local and regional problems and create new strategies which will favorably impact our climate. This is a good thing. However, I am concerned the same thing will happen with this legislation that happened with other federal legislation signed off by Biden-massive theft and fraud by the applicants. This will most certainly be the result if the agencies responsible for the distribution of the money do not do the proper planning and establish the proper controls to make theft unattractive. I predict that this will not happen because it never has or will. This makes it a bad thing.

Coal production before the war in Ukraine had declined 24.2 %. Coal jobs lost since 2019 totaled 10,645. Coal now supports only 20% of electricity produced in this country. Natural gas continues to replace coal simply because it is cheaper to produce. Coal companies had stopped investing in their companies. They were expecting the inevitable end. With the Russian invasion of Ukraine and the resulting disruption of energy markets, coal production in the U.S. has surged. Energy experts predict that coal will return to its former production levels when the war ends. The coal companies are hiring but are not investing. Most people think this is a good thing for the environment. I do as well. Let us face it, coal is one dirty mineral. It is a crime that China continues to build coal powered energy plants on a weekly basis in that huge country.

The next few paragraphs, I believe, are the real reasons why we cannot seem to cross that threshold which would allow us to make environmental progress. The industrialists in this country simply will not allow it.

- The shale boom early in the 21st century has reduced the federal deficit by 309 billion dollars in the last decade.

- North Dakota now produces 1.1 million barrels of oil a day. Oil is now at 90 dollars a barrel. Do the math. There is shale production in thirty states. There are 2.8 million jobs in place nationwide. Over a trillion dollars have gone into state and federal treasuries.

- We are a net exporter of liquefied natural gas (LNG); fifteen billion cubic meters will be shipped to Europe alone in 2022.

- The LNG industry has created thousands of well-paying jobs in an expanding market.

- Oil Change International released a report on September 12, 2023, confirming the United States will account for one-third of all planned oil and gas exploration across the globe from now until 2050, more than any other nation. U.S. crude oil exports have gone up 85% since the export ban was lifted in 2015.

The fossil fuel proponents and many Republicans remind Biden and his progressive friends in Congress that natural gas is not a renewable energy source. They also remind Biden that this product provides thousands of jobs and millions upon millions of dollars to state and federal coffers and to the general economy.

(The anti-fossil fuel activists do not have the power and they are not going to get it. They can riot all they want. The industrialists have the power and will not give it up. This country alone has a hundred-year supply of oil and gas that we know about. It will be consumed. And there you have it. MLR)

On May 8, 2022, the state of California generated enough power from renewables to meet 103% of consumer demand that day. What a remarkable achievement! State officials made it clear there is a lot of work to do on transmission and power storage issues. Renewable energy accounts for 29% of U.S. electricity production. This is a good thing.

In Brazil, deforestation and logging operations in the Amazon are down by 34% in a six-month period- January-June 2023. There has been a major crackdown on the corrupt players in that region. This gives the region, vital to the mitigation of carbon gases, a chance of recovery. If this is true, this is a good thing. Corruption is widespread there and has traditionally allowed major abuses in the management of the Amazon Basin. Greed vs. global climate salvation. Who will win?

Alberta, Canada recently hit the pause button on new renewable energy projects-118 projects worth thirty-three billion dollars. Carbon offsets worth billions of dollars were thought to be an effective strategy to combat climate issues. The government and industry in that province now consider them worthless. Carbon offsets in the U.S. have proven to be controversial as well. This is adding up to a bad thing because it was thought to be a sound financial strategy concept. Apparently, it is not in some circles. Time will tell.

In April 2023 Congress passed and Biden signed a 2.3-billion-dollar piece of legislation modernizing the National Power Grid. Long overdue. This is a good thing.

In the spring of 2023, Biden invoked the Defense Production Act to spur domestic mining of minerals used in batteries for Electric Vehicles (EVs). This was a very smart move because China now has a monopoly over the possession and production of these rare minerals. If China is angry with us for any reason down the road, getting those materials could and would be impossible to acquire.

Five billion dollars will be made available for investment in Lithium battery production. This is a good thing,

What is the insurance industry doing about climate control? The climate crisis is a financial crisis for most major insurers. You know this if you live near an ocean. In 2022, we sold a condominium we owned in Florida for thirty-three years. We sold it for many good reasons, the biggest was the fact we were just getting too old for it. The second major reason was the cost of ownership. Our home insurance had almost tripled in the last three years of ownership because we lived next to the ocean. On May 24, 2023, State Farm Insurance, the largest insurance company in the great state of California, will no longer insure homes in that state. Companies are raising rates, restricting coverage, or pulling out of states altogether. In Florida, most insurers have left. In Los Angeles, CA, the city is offering insurance companies millions of dollars in subsidies to come back. A major industry is under the guns because its business model is being destroyed by climate change. This is a bad thing.

In the U. S. today, 3.3 million people work in the clean energy sector. California has 500,000 employed, Texas has 250,000 employees followed by New York and Florida. Massachusetts ranks seventh in clean energy jobs with 118,165 employed, 3 % of all residents employed in that state. This is all good news, but the numbers must increase significantly in the next ten years across this country if we are to claim any progress in bringing positive change to our climate.

On October 11, 2023, the federal government announced the award of seven billion dollars to create seven regional hubs around the country to make and use hydrogen, a clean fuel that produces no planet warming emissions. Hydrogen releases only water vapor. The idea is to develop an entire industry from scratch.

Money will be awarded to seven hubs around the country. "Right now," hydrogen powers nothing in this country. By 2030, the goal is to produce ten million tons per year. The hubs have been identified: the Gulf Coast, Mid-Atlantic, Appalachia, Midwest, Upper Midwest, Pacific Northwest, and California. This is a good thing.

Sadly, the Willow Project in Alaska, mentioned previously, is just one of hundreds of oil and gas extraction projects recently approved throughout the world. And hundreds more are pending approval. Rystad Energy, a research firm, has documented that demand for fossil fuels is high everywhere. The production of natural gas is booming worldwide; fracking is playing a key role in that process. Trillions of dollars are now being invested in fossil fuel infrastructure that will become functional by the end of this decade, the same decade that many experts thought would be the point of no return for world climate stabilization. This year alone, major oil and gas exploration projects have been approved in Guyana, Brazil and Uganda, all oil rich countries. Coal dependent countries like South Africa, Vietnam, and Indonesia still rely heavily on coal and will for decades to come. In China, coal is still king. New coal powered energy plants come online on a weekly basis and there is nothing anyone can do about it. In Qatar, the world's largest gas production facility will come online in 2025. This plant will enable Qatar to increase its LNG production by 30%. After the pandemic was declared over, demand for oil and gas came roaring back, forcing companies to cancel or postpone renewable energy projects and, instead, increase oil and gas production capacity. In 2022, governments worldwide spent seven trillion dollars on oil and gas drilling. Who is kidding who?

Proposals

- No fossil fuel projects approved after December 31, 2024. This is wishful thinking but is absolutely necessary if goals set for the end of this decade have any chance of success. If Trump is President, you can forget it. If Biden is President, you can forget it. You just do not know what he is going to do. I think the real issue will be who controls the U.S. Congress. The Democrats will be a lot more active on climate change legislation and enforcement than the Republicans.

- Establish regional Climate Action centers to manage regional climate projects. The Inflation Reduction Act and other climate related legislation provide massive funding which would make this type of approach feasible. I would rather have regional and state level organizations doing the ground work and supervision than federal level bureaucrats.

- Pass federal legislation which will limit this country's annual Climate Change contribution to developing countries to one hundred million dollars annually. This is necessary to let developing countries and the world understand that the United States can no longer afford it because of its outlandish domestic debt which, by the middle of FY 2024, will be in the range of 38 trillion dollars (my estimate), up from the current debt of 33+ trillion dollars.

Michael L. Roeder

Chapter 7: War

(With the outbreak of war in Israel on October 7, 2023, the initial paragraphs written below are almost obsolete. The invasion of Israel by Hamas makes the stakes extremely high. Anything is possible. MLR)

"Right now," the stakes are high. However, this cannot only be about the war in Ukraine, although most of us look to Ukraine first when we wonder where that conflict may lead globally. Certainly, another war on the European continent involving this country cannot be ruled out. There is also Taiwan and China, North Korea and her neighbors Japan and South Korea, the Horn of Africa countries that have known nothing but warfare, famine, and flooding for decades, and South America and the many countries on that continent that have become corrupt military dictatorships with improving ties to Russia.

Warfare far more destructive than what we are seeing in Ukraine is a distinct possibility in the current environment. Russia's use of a tactical nuclear weapon in Ukraine would compel a major reaction from NATO and spark another conflict on the European continent. Biden is committed to keep funding the Ukraine effort although the "Continuing Resolution" passed by Congress and signed by the President on September 30, 2023, did not include any funding for Ukraine. A final budget for FY 2024, if there ever is one, should include funding but if it does not, other countries currently on the fence over future funding will take a powder and this could prove fatal for Ukraine's war effort.

The situation in Israel could become a long and deadly drawn-out affair, especially if Israel goes into Gaza. There is a strong feeling that Hezbollah will invade Israel in the north, which is forcing the United States to bring its air and sea power into play just in case. The U. S. Navy is already positioned in the Eastern Mediterranean with two aircraft carriers loaded with our best fighter jets. U. S. troops on the ground in Israel, let alone Gaza, cannot be in the cards unless Iran does something stupid. If Biden sends troops into Israel for humanitarian purposes only, Iran will not buy it and react. Time will tell.

There are other situations to consider as well. China is expanding its international interests in Africa and South America with massive loans and economic aid. Its expanding presence in the South China Seas has caused great concern around the world: Russia in Belarus and Putin's recent meetings with the leaders of China and North Korea do not bode well for peace loving countries; ISIS is still active in many countries in the Middle East; Al-Shabaab is a threat in Somalia and other countries on the Horn of Africa.

(China is everywhere with loans, military construction projects in Cuba, Djibouti, Angola, Pakistan, Sri Lanka, military aid, and infrastructure projects across the South Pacific. In the loan department, Ecuador got 4.5 billion dollars, Solomon Islands got sixty-six million dollars, Djibouti got 1.5 billion dollars, Angola got forty billion dollars, and Pakistan got thirty billion dollars. MLR)

The United States has the land, air, and sea power to meet any challenge. We have the best weapons systems money can buy. I do wonder if we can meet more than one challenge at the same time-sending a force to Europe to fight side by side with Ukraine forces against Russia and sending a force to Taiwan to defend against a Chinese attack. Or coming to Israel's aid if things go bad in Gaza. When I was on active duty, we had such a capability, and it was enormously expensive.

In 2022, none of the U. S. military services met its recruitment goals. The same was true for FY 2023. Many National Guard and U.S. Army Reserve (USAR) units are under strength. Many would-be recruits fail the services' entry level tests. They score poorly on aptitude tests because they have limited reading and comprehension skills. They cannot pass the army enlistment physical because they are overweight and in overall poor physical condition. They fail the run, cannot do the required push-ups and sit-ups. They have criminal records that cannot be waived for enlistment. It amounts to a national disgrace. Recruiters have stated publicly that they cannot recruit qualified individuals in many cases because they are not interested in putting up with all the "woke" bullshit that is currently infecting the country's armed forces. It is certainly a good thing that this country is not currently at war with anybody, although we have personnel stationed in over one hundred countries "Right now" and many serve under threat of actual combat.

Another serious and emerging issue is our ability to replenish our weapons stocks, especially missiles of all types, and supply Ukraine and Israel with weapons systems and munitions they need on a recurring basis. The New York Post did an article on this very issue on October 14, 2023. The article noted that our current production capability has been stretched thin from more than eighteen months of supplying Ukraine with all types of weapons systems, including missile systems which are currently the major weapons used by Ukraine and Russia in the war. Artillery is the dominant weapons system used by both sides. The former cold war production protocols are insufficient to meet current needs-our own, Ukraine, and Israel for starters. Ukraine alone will need 1.5 million shells for the next twelve months of fighting. We gave Ukraine 2 million shells as of July 2023. In January of 2023 we were producing 14,500 shells a month. "Right now," production has doubled. The plan is to produce 100,000 shells a month in 2025 at the cost of hundreds of millions of dollars just for shells.

Michael L. Roeder

According to the article, the Center for Strategic and International Studies (CSIS) released a report recently that indicated the U.S. would fire five thousand long range anti-ship missiles in the first week of war with China. It takes two years to build one of these missiles and China has control of the "rare earth metals" needed to build this type of missile. This is truly frightening.

In the case of China, at some point in time, that country will move against Taiwan. It is inevitable. The United States will have to respond as will South Korea and Japan. This is war no matter how you define the term. If by some miracle, China changed its position on Taiwan and allowed the country to remain independent as it is now, then the threat of war over Taiwan is eliminated. This is a long shot "Right now." China and the United States are not getting along very well now.

In the case of North Korea, the leader of that country, Kin Jung-un, is unpredictable which makes him a serious threat. He has developed close ties with China over the years and his recent visit to Russia represents a new "Axis of Evil," Russia, China, North Korea, and Iran.

In the case of Russia, if you take a serious look at NATO's actions since the collapse of Communism in the former Soviet Union in 1990, we have only ourselves to blame for Russia's invasion of Ukraine. Putin felt he had just cause to invade Ukraine. He was not a fan of Russia's demise as a world power. His invasion of the Crimea in 2014 showed him that he could invade another country and get away with it, just like Hitler did in 1938. The sad fact is that the United. States and NATO assured Russia it would not expand eastward towards that country, but that is exactly what it did. By 1999, NATO had admitted Hungary, Poland and the Czech Republic into the fold. By 2004, NATO had admitted seven more countries from Eastern Europe into the fold. By this time, Putin had taken firm control of Russia and was turning the country into his personal piggy bank. In 2008, NATO announced it intended to admit Ukraine and Georgia into NATO. In 2009, the United States announced it would position missiles in Poland and Romania. These missiles would be facing Russia. In 2014, Russia invaded the Crimea, a part of Ukraine, and in 2016 the United States began a buildup of troops in Europe. On February 24, 2022, Russia invaded Ukraine. We are now witnessing, daily, the carnage and destruction Russia has wrought on Ukraine. It is a war that could spiral out of control at any time. In the last few months, over Russia's strong objection, Finland has been admitted into NATO and Sweden soon will be. Take that Vladimir!!

It was initially thought that sanctions imposed by the United States and other countries would play a significant role in crippling Russia's ability to wage war in Ukraine. Since the invasion, Russia and Belarus have certainly suffered from sanctions but not to the point where they are in danger of losing this conflict. Russian Central Bank funds in the hundreds of millions of dollars have been frozen. Russian financial institutions have been cut off from the Global Swift Finance System, the international banking system. The Oligarchs loyal to Putin have had their yachts and planes, trains, and mansions located outside Russia seized. Despite it all, Russia is in it for the long haul.

Unbelievably, a New York Times article in the July 28, 2023, edition described the sanctions process currently in play in the United Kingdom. In Britain, Russian Oligarchs are allowed to spend hundreds of thousands of dollars on rewards while their bank accounts are frozen. Exceptions from sanctions are called "licenses." Eighty-two licenses were granted to these Oligarchs living in England in 2022. In effect, England is protecting these individuals. They should all be in jail because they are all crooks. This policy hurts the war effort against Russia in Ukraine because it reflects a lack of solidarity with its allies and Ukraine. On March 25, 2023, the World Bank estimated that the latest damage assessment in Ukraine at 411 billion dollars and growing as the war drags on. On March 18, 2023, the International Monetary Fund (IMF) approved a loan of 15.6 billion dollars just to keep the Ukraine economy afloat, an economy that has shrunk by a third since the invasion. Seven million people living in Ukraine now live in poverty.

Military Posture

I did a little research (actually a lot of research) on the military force compositions of the major countries I have been writing about-The United States, Russia, China, North Korea, South Korea, Japan, Iran, Israel, and Hamas. The information developed left me numb. There is so much destructive power on the table, available to good and evil people; one mistake could spell doom for all of us.

I looked at the force structure of each country: personnel, equipment in terms of planes, tanks, artillery and ships, nuclear weapons, and budgets. You should get the picture from all this data, which is only a small part of the total military story.

Ukraine Conflict

Country	U.S.	Ukraine	Russia
Budget	$842 B	$30.8 B	$86.3 B
Active Duty	1.4 M	700,000	1,190,000
Reserves	817,000	900,000	1,500,000
Navy Ships	296	N/A	267
Tanks	2,645	Limited*	1,800
Artillery	4,243	Limited	6,080
Nukes	5,244	N/A	5,943
Air	1,574	Limited	1,153

*Limited categories are supplied by U.S. and NATO countries. Tank inventory is rising as more soldiers are trained. Artillery pieces/shells are in great demand; production is not keeping up with demand. Air

Force fighter jets are increasing in number. Training of pilots is a major constraint "Right now."

Ukraine has received over one hundred billion dollars in military aid (money and equipment) from the U.S. since the invasion in February 2022. The power projection so far in this conflict has favored Ukraine and the enormous difference has been the military aid from supporting countries. Putin thought that Ukraine would be conquered in about a week. Twenty-one months later, November 2023, the war is stalemated. Putin should be worried and Zelensky is very worried because his forces cannot win unless the military aid from several supporting NATO countries keeps rolling in, in very big numbers. "Right now," the U.S. is a major supplier to Ukraine. There are plenty of American troops just west of Ukraine border. If they become a factor, then that means all hell has broken loose and that is when the numbers here will come into play. The U.S. helps Ukraine. Several NATO countries, Poland immediately, will enter the fray. Who helps Putin? Belarus will have no choice, but the country is weakened by corruption and a very unhappy populace which would rise in revolt if Belarus sent troops into Ukraine to help the Russians. The people of Belarus hate their leader, Aleksander Lukashenko, with a passion. In an all-out conflict, I humbly suggest that Ukraine will win in a short war.

(I will state this one more time, briefly. If corruption scandals continue to surface in Ukraine, Zelensky and his regime could be finished. This in turn could lead to diminished funding for the war effort and give some leaders the perfect excuse to get out and save a lot of money. Also, if Trump runs and is elected, I believe he will stop or fatally reduce military aid to Ukraine in a heartbeat. MLR)

Taiwan

Country	Taiwan	Japan	S. Korea	China	N. Korea	U.S.
Budget	$19.1 B	$51 B	$46.3 B	$291 B	Unknown	$842 B
Active Duty	290,00	250,000	625,000	2.8 M	1.3 M	1.4 M
Reserves	1.6 M	50,000	3 M	1.1 M	600,000	817,000
Navy Ships	136	155	160	348	470	296
Tanks	1,100	540	2,872	5,250	4,200	2,645
Artillery	1,116	500	5,800	7,094	6,000	4,243
Nukes	None	None	Unknown	419	20	5,244
Air	741	330	160	3,260	899	1,574

In WWII, the Japanese held Pacific Islands about to be invaded were first bombed by American airpower for 2-5 days before the land invasion began. On some islands, our troops landed without a shot being fired initially. On other islands, the American forces were often met with heavy artillery and land fire before they hit the landing zones. Taiwan is an island. I have no idea what the Taiwanese army will do in defense of the country. Whatever happens, it will not be pretty. China will open with a heavy surprise bombing of key military and government structures, Air Force and Navy installations and then follow that with a massive sea invasion. China has the resources to do that kind of maneuver in spades. I doubt the land invasion will be a surprise because Taiwan has excellent intelligence capability and would be able to detect large troop movements from China. Or China just might use a tactical nuclear device for a knockout punch before any help arrives from Japan, South Korea, or the United States. You must give China an edge here, although Taiwan has a very well trained and equipped force structure that could give China and its main ally, North Korea, a lot of grief before it is over.

Israel and Hamas and Hezbollah

Country	Israel	Hamas	Hezbollah	Iran
Budget	$23.4 B	Unknown	$1 B	Unknown
Active Duty	169,500	90,000	25,000	610,000
Reserves	465,000	10,000	20,000	359,000
Navy Ships	49	None	None	56
Tanks	2,200	Thousands	150,000	1,000
Artillery	530	None	Missiles	2,900
Nukes	90	None	None	Unknown
Air	339	None	None	300

The U.S. will stay with Israel as long as Biden is President of this country. The financial burden it will create on our federal budget will be enormous. If the U. S. sends ground troops in any form, there will be the danger of an expanded conflict in that region because of Iran's reaction to U.S. troops on the ground. The people who control Iran are demons in religious garments. They are fanatical and instill fanaticism in everyone they control, including Hamas in Gaza and Hezbollah in Lebanon. They will not hesitate to attack American and/or Israeli forces even if they know they will die and lose in the process. They want to die. There will be no peace negotiations on this one. Israel knows that any peace will be fleeting and that Hamas will invade again in due time, a year from now, fifteen years from now, it doesn't matter to these people. They have great patience. The exact same for Hezbollah in Lebanon. Israel has one of the best trained, best funded armies in the world. "Right now," Gaza City in northern Gaza is mostly destroyed. The entire state has been bombed and softened up for the Israeli invasion which has been slow in coming but it is coming. The force structure favors Israel even if Iran enters the fray with ground forces. History also favors Israel. They have been in Gaza several times in the last twenty years in response to previous terror attacks. They have the Gaza Strip in a lockdown. They have cut off water, electricity, food, hospital supplies and still some believe it is all for show. A million Palestinians in Gaza are on the move south to the Egyptian border in the hope of getting out to go where-the United States? I would not bet on it. "Right now," 2 Republican Congressmen, Rep. Tom Tiffany(R-WIS) and Rep. Andy Ogles(R-TENN) have submitted legislation titled: "Guaranteeing Aggressors Zero Admissions Act", which will prohibit any person holding a Palestinian passport entry into the United States. It is being called the "Gaza Act." Egypt does not want them, which is why the only exit out of Gaza to Egypt is closed. A million people at the border with no food, water, health care or a place to sleep. The humanitarian disaster that is sure to follow in the weeks ahead will go down as one of the worst in recorded history, ironically ranked just below the Holocaust in WWII. The stark reality is that Israel will have to go house to house in Gaza to flush out the actual enemy who by now have mostly discarded their uniforms and put on their Sunday best with the hope they survive for another day. Casualty rates on both sides will be high but both sides realize this. And who will rebuild Gaza when this war is over? How about Saudi Arabia, Bahrain, Qatar, and the other oil rich countries in the Middle East watching this debacle from a distance.

(Shortly after writing this chapter, Israel went into Gaza and all hell has broken loose. The Gaza Strip is being destroyed inch by inch with intensive bombings daily, ground assaults with heavy tank support on suspected Hamas positions and the execution of a well-planned offense which has resulted in over 25,000 dead, 50,000 wounded Palestinians and 155 Israeli soldier deaths. IDF is claiming thousands of Hamas fighters have been killed. Palestinians are paying a huge price for the Hamas strategy of using civilian facilities

like hospitals for command centers and staging areas. One thing is clear, there will be no cease fire and Hamas is through. If there is any pause in the fighting, it will be connected to a hostage agreement. The pause will be brief but if it is not, Israel has screwed itself. I would not be surprised if Israel at some point in this war goes into Southern Lebanon and wipes out Hezbollah. After that is done, the West Bank should be paid a visit and Mr. Abbas should be sat down and explained how the West Bank will behave in the future. MLR)

(On November 21, 2023, a hostage agreement was ironed out. Fifty Israeli hostages would be released in exchange for 150 Palestinian women and children currently in Israeli prisons. Hundreds of trucks loaded with food, medical supplies, and fuel, would be allowed into Gaza. There would be a four day pause in the fighting. For every ten additional hostages released by Hamas, the pause would be extended for one day. The key word is pause. Hamas must be wiped out; Hezbollah must be wiped out. Pause is good but not great for Israel. They may not fully understand how the progressive mind works. This agreement will be considered a sign of weakness by Hamas and their left wing progressive liberal friends if the pause goes from 4 days to say two weeks. And they will do everything they can to extend this pause until it becomes a truce. The Progressives in the U.S. failed. The IDF assault resumed on November 30, 2023, with increased vigor. Make no mistake about it. Hamas is through in Gaza once and for all. MLR)

Proposals

There are no proposals.

Of the ten chapters covered in this book, this chapter (Chapter Seven) is the most important. It is the one area of concern that mandates the attention of the most powerful and positioned leaders in the world to work on solutions and that is the problem. The United States government is stepping up to the plate. Biden and his progressives are putting heavy pressure on Israeli leadership to come to terms and end hostilities AFTER the hostage negotiations run their course. Indeed, the U.N. condemned the Hamas attack and then came out with a weak-kneed statement saying Israel was breaking the law by shutting off power, water and food to the Gaza Strip. That certainly fell on deaf ears because everyone is well aware that Israel is going to obliterate Hamas and Hezbollah as well, if Hezbollah gets involved. Quite frankly, Israel could care less if they are breaking any laws. They feel that their country is at risk of destruction by these terrorist groups and, after seventy-five years of putting up with this Muslim bullshit, they are finally going to do something about it permanently. The stark reality that many Jews and Palestinians are going to be killed and injured is nothing more than the cost of warfare and, while it is heartbreaking to see Jewish and Palestinian children dying on national TV, we have seen exactly this happen in all the previous world wars and regional conflicts in recorded history.

Chapter 8: The Economy

It is the economy, the world economy, which will provide the funding to solve, or at least manage out of crisis, most of the issues discussed in this book.

Any economy that produces the funding would have to involve all the industrialized countries that would put people to work to produce the goods and services necessary to provide the government funds and resources to confront the monumental problems the world population faces today. The goal is to raise enough tax dollars to fund international, national, and regional goals. At this point in time, I do not believe the political will exists to do that. A case in point is the United States of America, a country so deeply in debt- today it is 33 trillion, 800 billion, 780 million dollars and growing-it is inconceivable that the country, in the future, will have the resources to deal effectively with the drug scourge, crime and corruption, the national debt, climate control, immigration, national defense, the list is endless. Many other countries, rich and poor, face the same dilemma. Outpacing revenue flows is the road to disaster and that is what is happening right now across the globe.

In the United States, our current political system is paralyzed. It is November 2023, and we do not have a FY 2023-2024 federal budget. We are two months into the new fiscal year, and we do not have a budget. We do have a Continuing Resolution that ends in a few days. At that point, we have a budget or another Continuing Resolution or the U.S. government shuts down just in time for the holidays.

Michael L. Roeder

(On November 15, 2023, a second CR was passed. Four appropriation bills were funded through January19, 2024 and eight appropriation bills were funded through February 2, 2024. It turns out Johnson has the same problems McCarthy had - zombie like far-right wing Republicans - and Johnson is a committed MAGA lover. MLR)

We now have a brand new MAGA loving Speaker of the House in the House of Representatives, Mike Johnson of Louisiana, who credits God for all his good fortune. His election comes after Kevin McCarthy of California was ousted by a few radical Republican House Representatives who sided with blood thirsty Democrats to oust him and cause the Congress to shut down just as Israel was invaded and Ukraine was pleading for more military support. We do deserve better than this, don't you think?

This is no way to run and finance government operations, especially when you are the most powerful and wealthiest country in the world. The very people who were elected to manage this country have instead engaged in cheap partisan political behavior to the point where nothing is getting done. This means that the economy will fail as quickly as the government fails and our national government is failing. All the recent polls, whether conducted by liberal or conservative organizations, show that, on average, 70% of Americans polled believe that the country is heading in the wrong direction; 70% of Americans do not want to see Biden and Trump in a presidential contest; and a majority of Americans polled would vote for a third party candidate if given that option. This may be the right time for a third party to emerge, but it would have to put forward a viable slate of candidates to be successful. The "No Labels Party" must get off the couch and commit a slate. Robert Kennedy, now running as an independent candidate, will take votes away from Biden and Trump but I do not believe he will be a factor in the race. No matter how you look at it, it is bad for America. It is clear to me that the 2024 presidential election is the most important election in this country's history.

(I said the same thing about the 2012 election and the 2016 election and the 2020 election, but I was wrong three times. I am not wrong about this election. MLR)

A well-funded third party with a solid slate of candidates is needed. At least, the average American voter will have a real choice. Biden vs. Trump is a doomsday scenario for this country. This election, with a well-funded third-party slate, has the possibility of bringing moderation back to the political process.

(November 7th, 2023, was Election Day in this country. In my hometown, there were a number of important races for Mayor, the city council, and other offices. Westfield has 26, 561 registered voters, the vast majority being un-enrolled. A grand total of 5,930 voters went to the polls and voted for a mayoral candidate, about 22% of eligible voters. The incumbent Mayor won by a landslide but hardly anyone voted. This trend was reflected in other cities in the area. In Springfield, MA, a city of 150, 000 people ten miles from Westfield, the incumbent Mayor Sarno won a sixth term but only 21,022 residents voted, 19% of those eligible to vote. These numbers are pathetic. There was some good news that came out at the national level right after the election, however. Sen. Joe Manchin announced he was not running for re-election in his home state. Some political experts think he will be the presidential candidate for the No Labels Party that is posturing to announce a slate of third-party candidates. Let us hope so. MLR)

These poor turnouts cannot be the norm a year from now. If it is, this country is screwed because a third party will not prevail. A low turnout nationally will be a godsend for Trump and get him elected. I am hoping for a record turnout for 2024. That election is a final opportunity for the American people to end the bullshit happening in this country "Right now."

The proposed FY 2023-2024 budget stands at 6.9 trillion dollars. To fund it, additional borrowing will be required to meet financial goals. The Congressional Budget Office (CBO) estimates that the budget deficit for this budget will be 1.9 trillion dollars by the end of that fiscal year. If this holds true, this country achieves nothing except more debt. If this holds true, the national debt will grow to thirty-five trillion, six hundred billion dollars. The interest on that amount of money will exceed one trillion dollars for FY 2024!! What strikes fear in my heart is what Biden and his cronies want to do to raise most of this money: raise the corporate tax rate from 21 to 28%; raise the top individual tax rate from 37 to 39.6 %; institute a 25% minimum tax on people and families with a net worth of one hundred million dollars; institute a 15% minimum tax on billion-dollar companies and corporations no matter where they are headquartered; and the Medicare tax would go from 3.8 to 5% on income over 400,000 dollars. Most of this is crap. I do like the minimum corporate tax because it will force every corporation to pay something. The rest of it penalizes the rich and does nothing to stop the current, uncontrolled spending frenzy in play in this country. We are currently in the fifth month of that budget year with no budget. We do have another CR but what happens in February 2024?

Chapter 9: Summary

Immigration

The failure of the Biden Administration and the Congress to resolve our current immigration debacle is grounds for voters in this country to vote Biden out of office.

(On the day after Biden took office, the U.S. Citizenship Act 0f 2021 was introduced in the Congress with eighty co-sponsors. It was considered the most comprehensive reform immigration bill ever presented for consideration. It died in sub-committee along with several other immigration bills. This has been going on for a quarter century. One bill after another goes in the toilet. Who in the hell do these people in Congress think they are? They really do not represent a damn thing. MLR)

A resolution of this serious issue, immigration reform, is needed "Right now," not over the next decade. Trillions of dollars will be required to deal with the millions of undocumented immigrants already in this country and the millions who will arrive in the next few years. The fact is they will never stop coming. And they come with nothing, no money, limited skills, no health insurance, no jobs, minimal education, lots of kids and little mastery of the English language. They will require support for years to come.

(In a New York Times article, posted on November 11, 2023, former Trump supporters gave the paper an extensive interview on

Trump's 2025 immigration plan if he is elected. Most of it they contend can be implemented without legislative action and it will be put into play immediately after he is sworn in. Here are the highlights. MLR)

- Round up undocumented immigrants already in this country on a grand scale and detain them until they are expelled.

(I support this because it will end the invasion of people who we cannot support any longer. This effort will require the mobilization of all our resources, civilian and military, to be successful. MLR)

- Invoke COVID-19 era policy to refuse asylum claims and expel undocumented immigrants. Title 42 would come roaring back.

(I support this because it worked effectively under Trump's presidency. The asylum claim strategy used by migrants was and is a huge fraud. MLR)

- Keep Muslims out.

(I do not support this. I do support increased monitoring of VISA applicants for Muslims from most Muslim countries wanting to enter this country for any reason. This would include Muslim students accepted for study at our premier universities and colleges. Visas of foreign university students who supported the recent pro-Palestinian demonstrations nationwide would be cancelled and the students sent home where they belong. Applicants from Iran, Iraq and Lebanon would be denied. MLR)

- Finish the border wall.

(I support this only if enough enforcement assets are allocated to monitor the wall. "Right now," it is obvious that extensive stretches of the wall are not covered because immigrants are having a field day getting by it, through it and over it. MLR)

- Temporary Protected Status for immigrants, which allows immigrants in this country to work would be canceled.

(I do not support. This is where Trump goes off the rails. Allowing immigrants in this country legally (fully vetted) is a win-win for everyone. MLR)

- Birthright citizenship would be ended.

(I support this. Immigrants in this country legally or illegally, are eligible for welfare benefits by virtue of having a child born in this country. It costs the taxpayers of this country billions of dollars annually. We can no longer afford this cost. It must end. This is a genuine issue which can only be resolved by legislative action, so nothing will be done in the immediate future. If Biden wins, forget it. If Trump wins, it will depend on the structure of the new Congress. If Manchin wins, it is a possibility and will depend on the structure of the new Congress. MLR)

- End the Deferred Action for Childhood Arrivals (DACA).

(I do not support this. During the Obama administration, he tried to pass legislation to give these children, brought into the country illegally by their parents, a path to citizenship. The Congress would not buy it. Trump would end the repeated attempts to pass this legislation. This would subject hundreds of thousands, over a million immigrants, to deportation. Studies have shown that most of these children, now adults, have made great progress in this country. To subject them to expulsion would be a big mistake. MLR)

- Bar visitors from troubled foreign countries.

(I support this. The definition of "Troubled" should not be too difficult. Russia would be one. Iran would be another. Belarus would be another. How about Yemen, Sudan, Venezuela, Sri Lanka, Syria,

and so on. It would be interesting to see what the list would like under the Trump administration. MLR)

- Expedited removal of undocumented aliens under the Alien Enemies Act of 1798. This act would be used against suspected cartel members and drug gangs.

(I support this. Who would not? MLR)

Law enforcement personnel from all levels of government would be brought to the southern border to enforce this policy. Stephen Miller, the architect of Trump's immigration policy back in 2016 and the lead on this new policy, indicated that most of these proposals will not require legislative action. We will see about that. The point is that many people in this country, including me, will vote for Trump or anyone who supports an immigration policy like this because we all know by now that Biden will not change a damn thing and the Congress, as it exists now, cannot do a damn thing about anything.

At some point soon, we have to say, "enough is enough." At some point we have to say the borders are closed at some number. We must send many of them back to their country of origin. We do not and never will have enough revenue to cover the cost of sustaining these people, who now come to our shores by hook or by crook from just about every country worldwide.

("Right now," there are thousands of migrants walking across Mexico towards El Paso, Texas. This would be a good starting point to turn them back once they arrive in El Paso. We should all follow this one closely because from this march many thousands more will come if we do nothing. MLR)

The next election must be the singular event which changes this phenomenon. Biden will not, Trump will. Regarding the new Congress, who knows? If anyone is expecting legislation to set positive immigration policy for this country, forget it in the short term. The current Congress has polio, there is no federal budget, and many states are hopelessly in debt. Americans have every right to be concerned and pissed off at the same time. There is presently a pervasive feeling of sadness, a sense of heightened frustration and anger in this country over the state of the Union. I feel it every day and I know I am not alone. In Europe it is called "Eco-anxiety."

(The progressives responsible for this mess are not just found in abundance at the federal level of government. Massachusetts has always been a liberal bastion. The state Legislature has been dominated for years by liberal Democrats. Currently, of the two hundred seats in the Senate and the House of Representatives, 170 are Democrats. What kept things sane was the tendency of voters to elect a Republican governor. That changed in 2020 when a Democratic governor was elected, and the legislature stayed predominantly Democrat. This is noteworthy because Massachusetts is by state law a "Right to Shelter" state, the only one in the country. Its 7,500 beds allocated for the homeless and immigrants are filled and waiting lists are now being developed as migrants flood into the state with nowhere to go. The State of Massachusetts has money in the bank. Recently, excess tax revenues, over a billion dollars, were distributed to residents and another billion dollars plus was put in the bank for a rainy day, which has arrived. The state currently has a five billion dollar surplus and a debt of seventy-six billion dollars. Governor Maura Healey is pleading with the feds to send the state a couple of hundred million dollars to cover anticipated costs just to house the undocumented immigrants coming soon. Fat chance that will happen any time soon. In the meantime, in her quest to find additional community beds, she has decided that a vacant dormitory on the campus of Westfield State University (WSU), just a mile from my home, would be an ideal place to house 350 immigrants coming from Haiti. This has met with almost universal resistance from local politicians and even the

university administration as well. Not to mention a ton of parents who are furious that these immigrants will be living in the middle of the campus several miles from any services. To deal with this potential problem at WSU and other places, the governor called up 250 National Guardsmen to be available to get these people to the doctor, the library, the supermarket, the movies, whatever. No immigrants have yet to be housed at WSU, but it is going to happen. State officials inspected the dormitory in October 2023 and found it suitable. MLR)

The fact is that there is not enough money in the world to take care of this monumental social problem. Much of the world is on the move due to climate change, corruption, warfare, and lack of opportunity. Our economy cannot sustain, is not sustaining the immigration problem in this country. Countrywide, states, and cities are drowning in debt as they try to deal with the ever-increasing number of undocumented immigrants being let into this country by a liberal, progressive administration headed by Joe Biden, who seems tone deaf to the chaos that exists.

The Drug Scourge

The world and this country face a drug scourge so out of control despite herculean efforts by global law enforcement organizations to manage the problem. The reason is simple: demand is out of control. The United States over the last fifty years has spent hundreds of billions of dollars to manage this problem and it has only gotten worse. In this country, the solution cannot be tied to increasing funding because we do not have the money. The solution just might be the legalization of all drugs and let this country go to hell in a hand basket because that is exactly where we are headed. I do not see a solution to this problem. I do see a possibility that this problem could be managed. The answer is not "Harm reduction." The answer is something I would never thought of supporting just a few years ago, but the arrival of fentanyl and xylazine has changed my position.

(As I am writing this, a television newscast announced that a one-year-old child being cared for in a Bronx, NY daycare facility was dead and three other children in critical condition after inhaling the drug fentanyl at the facility. What? Turns out that the police go into the place, fully approved and licensed by the city and recently inspected, and find large quantities of fentanyl, cocaine and xylazine and three "kilo" packing machines used to package large amounts of drugs. Also turns out that the owner and a tenant illegally in the country are arrested soon after for murder and an assortment of drug charges that should put them both in prison for life-you would think. The three babies involved, 16, 13 and 8 months, were taken to a hospital and revived with NARCAN which is used to treat fentanyl and opioid overdoses. The city employees who inspected the place should be fired. MLR)

This incident is a classic case that, if dealt with properly, would allow this country to manage the drug scourge to the point where it would be considered just a "Drug Problem."

First and foremost, the parties arrested are charged with the maximum charges, which they were.

Second, in cases of violence, there is no chance for a plea bargain. In this case, plea bargains are rare but do occur more than they should countrywide.

Third, in capital cases, no bail is allowed. Today, bail is the norm even in many capital cases. In cases where bail is allowed, it often comes with pre-trial conditions which are enforced by nobody in most cases.

Fourth, a speedy trial would occur and, if found guilty, alternate sentences like probation, community release, etc. are not allowed. Imprisonment is mandatory.

In cases where the individual is addicted to drugs, is not violent, is not on any type of court supervision like probation, a national diversion program for treatment should be offered. Failure to accept treatment upon initial screening would mean the same conditions as stipulated above. No bail, no plea bargaining and a speedy trial Imprisonment would be mandatory.

This modality would cost billions at the federal level and billions at the state level if states agreed with the federal strategy and pass enabling legislation at the state level. Federal subsidies would be required. The federal government would ultimately save billions of dollars a year if this type of program were established. I believe this approach, coupled with strong enforcement of federal and state drug laws, would reduce the drugs available and the number of active drug users on our streets.

The concept of bail could be a problem, especially in courts dominated by progressive judges. Bail under the Constitution is set to insure appearance in court. In today's crazy world, it should be used to protect the public safety and in some "Red" states that is exactly what happens. A constitutional amendment would be required to change the Constitution's intent. The chance of that ever happening is akin to me winning the Powerball Lottery. No matter what happens in the future, this drug problem we have will never go away. It is a management issue that can be executed successfully without causing a fiscal disaster.

The National Debt

At 33+ trillion dollars, this country's debt and the interest paid on that debt annually, is a dead weight on all of us. Several federal agencies and Non-Governmental Agencies (NGOs) have recently estimated that the national debt will increase to forty-eight trillion dollars by 2030 just due to legislation already on the books. By that time, much of the federal budget will be dedicated to the payment of mandatory government benefits-Social Security, retirements-federal and military, Medicare, and

Medicaid, to name just a few. There will be little room for discretionary spending and no room for unanticipated costs, like support of Ukraine and Israel, which alone has already cost the American taxpayer hundreds of billions of dollars and counting.

The struggle now in our Congress is the fight between the progressives on the far left and the conservatives on the far right over this very issue. Unfortunately, the Republican Party has been taken over by a bunch of right-wing idiots who refuse to budge on their demands for huge budget cuts starting with the 2024 budget.

Significant cuts are necessary but the progressives, led by President Biden, are in no mood to negotiate. In fact, for the FY 23-24 budget, in-your-face Biden spendocrats are proposing a budget totaling 6.9 trillion dollars that includes: a hefty tax on the wealthy (5.5 trillion dollars in tax increases in the next ten years to offset spending increases); 5.2% pay raise for federal employees/ military; 2.1 billion dollars for early childhood education; five billion dollars in election administration assistance; fifty-nine billion dollars in affordable housing spending; twenty-six billion dollars for border security; a 26-billion-dollar boost in defense spending; six billion dollars for Ukraine; three billion dollars to poor countries for global warming, just for starters.

(Since Biden took offices in 2021, the national debt has increased by five trillion dollars. If the FY 2023-24 budget, as presented by the House passes, the national debt will balloon by an estimated twenty trillion dollars over the next decade. This budget has little chance of making any progress in the House of Representatives as it is now constructed. It would be considered deadweight in the U. S. Senate. "Right now," which is the middle of November at this writing, the only solution to avoid a government shutdown is another Continuing Resolution. If it happens, it will be a classic case of kicking the can down the road. MLR)

(It happened. Another CR was passed on November 15 which keeps the government operating until the middle of January 2024. The House Republicans have a strategy which would allow them to exact severe budget cuts by bringing up the twelve major spending bills one at a time. Can you imagine the chaos that will erupt as each bill is discussed? There is a good chance this country will not have a federal budget passed for FY 2023-2024. It could be the year of Continuing Resolutions. Please keep this in mind as the November 2024 elections approach. MLR)

We can change this stalemate in Congress by voting these fools out when the time comes in November 2024, although I admit by that time it may be too late.

A third party, led by moderates, could develop an effective slate of challengers to run against these hapless incumbents. Just who are they?

Let us start with the Republicans.

Rep. Matt Gaetz-Florida: Loves Trump and underage girls. He is being investigated for some of his dates, but he is undeterred and has taken full responsibility for his role in getting Kevin McCarthy booted out as House Speaker. He wants huge budget cuts and had caused House paralysis until the recent election of Rep. Michael Johnson –Louisiana.

(Gaetz is facing problems in his home state because of his asinine behavior but "Right now" he has no opposition in the 2024 election. MLR)

Rep. Michael Johnson-Louisiana: recently elected Speaker of the House. A strong Trump supporter, he is nothing more than a Trump extremist waiting for Trump to return. Nothing could be worse for this country. This guy strongly advocated for the overturn of the 2020 election; he voted against the first Continuing Resolution which prevented a government shutdown; he supports huge spending cuts; he does not support continued funding for Ukraine or same sex marriage and celebrated the overturn of Roe vs. Wade. We can only hope the Democrats gain control of the House of Representatives in 2024. Don't we???

Rep. George Santos-New York: This character has survived two attempts by the House of Representatives to expel him for all his misdeeds which are too numerous to mention in this book. The first time, months ago, Kevin McCarthy saved his ass because, as Speaker of the House at the time, he did not want to potentially lose a seat in the House where the Republicans have a slim majority. The second time, on November 11, 2023, he got a break because his fellow representatives thought the fact that he is currently facing federal criminal charges and an investigation by the House Ethics Committee to boot, was sufficient to eventually guarantee his expulsion from the House and a lengthy prison term.

(The guy fabricated his life story, stole money from donors, lied to Congress and received unemployment benefits he did not deserve. The second vote did not even get a simple majority-30 Democrats voted against the measure. Why? Should anyone be surprised? Only 5 House members have been expelled in its history and three occurred during the Civil War! Santos plans to run for re-election in 2024. At least three individuals have announced their intention to run for the seat. MLR)

(Just in. On November 16, 2023, the House Ethics Committee issued a scathing report on Santos but made no recommendations, nothing. Santos did say after the report was released that he would not seek re-election, which means he gets to stay in Congress for another year. Complete bullshit. MLR)

(Thankfully, a movement is underway in the House of Representatives to expel this character, a move that has wide support on both sides of the aisle. It took the House Ethics Committee Report to get to this point. An expulsion vote could

happen by the end of November 2023. As I noted in Chapter 5, the U. S. House expelled him on December 1, 2023, by a significant margin. MLR)

Rep. Lauren Boebort-Colorado was re-elected in 2022 and has been a loose cannon since. Another MAGA lover, she voted to oust McCarthy and wants the big budget cuts as well. More importantly, the recent divorcee was with a date at a movie theater in Denver in November having a grand old-time vaping during the show, grabbing her dates genitals, her date grabbing her breasts. The management got a lot of complaints and the couple got kicked out of the theatre. The event went public with actual photos so there was no doubt as to what happened.

(As a result, Republicans in Colorado have had enough, and many have already endorsed Jeff Hurd to force a primary. On the Democratic side, Adam Frisch has announced a run for the seat. Boebort beat him in 2022 by just 546 votes. Both Hurd and Frisch are considered moderates. Boebort needs to go. MLR)

(On January 3, 2024, Boebert announced that she is going to run for re-election in a different district in November. She now represents Colorado's 3rd Congressional District; she will now run for the seat in the fourth district which is considered more heavily Republican. A week before the announcement, she and her ex-husband got into a hot verbal argument in a Colorado restaurant they had gone to, to make peace. Instead, they made war, and her ex accused her of punching him in the nose. However, a video of the incident proved that she was innocent. No arrests. This is a shout-out to the voters in Colorado's 4th Congressional District. Will a good, politically moderate resident run against this crazy person? Please. MLR)

Rep. Marjorie Taylor Greene-Georgia: elected in 2021, she is another loose cannon and MAGA lover. She is a January 6th conspiracy proponent, mis-information guru, anti-Muslim, anti-vaccine champion, and an overall jerk. She is running for re-election and has no challenger. The people of her district in Georgia need to wake up.

(Former President Donald Trump- true, he is not currently in office, but it looks like he will be in about 11 months or so. How can you leave him out of this conversation? I cannot. While in office he was impeached twice but not convicted. Out of office, he has been indicted four times and faces a total of ninety-one criminal counts in federal and state courts. He was sued successfully in civil court by a woman who claimed she was raped by this guy and was awarded millions. His real estate empire in New York is under threat in another civil action trial "Right now." MLR)

The Democrats

Sen. Robert Menendez-New Jersey: currently under federal indictment for influence peddling, acting illegally as an unregistered foreign agent, bribery along with his wife. This was a family affair. Menendez beat a federal charge several years ago with a hung jury. He is facing a lengthy prison term if convicted. He is running for re-election in 2024 but he will certainly have a number of challengers. On January 3, 2024, Menendez was hit with a superseded warrant from the eastern country of Qatar.

(Eventually we will be able to say, "Good Riddance," to this guy and his wife. It looks like the wife of the New Jersey governor has thrown her hat in the ring to run against Menendez in November. Others will be joining. MLR)

Rep. Alexandria Ocasio-Cortez-Bronx-Queens, NY: she is a member and leader of the "Squad," a left wing socialist leaning group of representatives who want nothing more than to cause the collapse of democracy in this country. Of all the socialist members of the Squad, she gets the most media coverage. She is anti-Semite, anti-everything

Democrat. She is presently running unopposed for re-election, but two individuals are preparing to challenge.

Rep. Rashida Tlaib- Michigan: the only Palestinian in Congress, she has condemned Israel for the invasion of Gaza. She is another anti-Semite in Congress and a big mouth troublemaker who cares little about Democracy in this country. She was censured by her House colleagues recently for a speech she gave on the Gaza War after she said, "all Israelis should be driven from the river to the sea." She is presently running for re-election unopposed.

Rep. Ayanna Pressley-Massachusetts: elected in 2019, she is up for re-election in 2024. She is a member of the "Squad." She is an anti-Semite who has taken her far left beliefs to new heights in a state where left wing beliefs prevail, at least in the eastern half of the state. She is running unopposed.

Rep. Ilan Omar-Minnesota: elected in 2019, she is up for re-election in 2024. She exists in Congress to cause turmoil. At the local level, she was a strong advocate to abolish the Minneapolis Police Department. She wants to abolish the Federal Immigration and Customs Enforcement Division. She advocated for an immediate cease fire in the Israel-Hamas war. She is another anti-Semite in Congress. She could give a damn about the welfare of this country. She is a member of the "Squad." Retired Minneapolis Councilman Don Samuels is weighing a rematch in 2024. Two other individuals are challenging Omar as well.

There are other Democrats in the House to be concerned about: Cori Bush, Missouri (will be opposed in a primary by Wesley Bell, St Louis County prosecutor); Jamaal Bowman, New York, the jerk who pulled the fire alarm during the House debate on the first Continuing Resolution to prevent a vote and cause the government to shut down. He was censured in early December 2023. He should have been expelled; Nydia Velasquez, New York, another anti-Semite socialist who condemned the Israel move into Gaza. She is running unopposed.

(While the 2024 elections are months away, it is appalling that many of these clowns are running unopposed "Right now". This must change for the good of this country. MLR)

Corruption

Corruption, as bad as it is in the United States, is at record levels of activity and exposure the world over. The worse thing our policy makers and politicians can do is to ignore the findings of organizations like Transparency International. Their findings should be embraced, and policy developed on their findings. The cost of passing more stringent laws and enforcing them will be costly and it may require resource shifting to make it work but we really have no choice. Republican presidential candidate Nikki Haley has said she will not give foreign aid money to any country which scores less than a fifty on the Transparency International Corruption Perception Index (CPI). If she is elected President of the United States and did that, based on the index scores published in 2022, 70% of the 180 countries rated annually, or 126 countries, would get no U.S. foreign aid, saving U.S. taxpayers billions of dollars annually. The biggest challenge will be to hire enough specialists in finance and accounting to enforce the laws in place. Transparency will be paramount. Regarding any type of aid this country hands out to the world in the future, countries in receipt of our financial support will have to open their ledgers for inspection by our auditors or forfeit that aid. The United Sates recently forced that issue in Ukraine, which is a hotbed of corruption even during all out conflict in that country. Now, our auditors can follow our money in that country to make sure it is used for the intended purpose. We must impress the corrupt leaders of these countries that stealing is simply not worth it. Regarding the money we give out to individuals and programs in this country, based on the scandals surrounding the theft of government dollars given out by the Biden administration in 2021 and 2022 amounting to trillions of dollars, we have a lot of work to do to get that same message out: "If you steal government funds you will get caught and will go to jail." "Right now," that is not happening enough to motivate people to play it straight.

In the U.S. Congress, for those countries that steal our foreign aid, military aid, economic aid, outright grants, I would suggest that we simply stop giving these countries anything for ten years and then let them reapply. As Jerry Seinfeld would say "Not that there's anything wrong with that." And it would save us untold billions of dollars annually.

Climate Change

In these early years of the 21st century, climate is acting up and acting out, destroying lives, economies, topography, crops, infrastructure of all types, habitats of all types and causing a worldwide sense of impending disaster. Storms are more powerful and destructive, rains more torrential or no rain falls at all for extended periods of time in many parts of the world. Fires are erupting everywhere that cause massive destruction not seen in decades. Entire rivers across the globe have dried up for good. Sea levels are rising, and water temperatures are increasing at accelerated rates. It is a tale of death, drought, famine, flood, severe air pollution and unpredictable weather patterns, all impacting the quality of our lives and causing widespread uncertainty about the future of our planet.

This is certainly bad news, but it is ironically also good news because this new weather/climate reality has impressed world leaders and good things are happening as a result. Substantial resources are being allocated to bring this possible world-ending scenario down to a manageable and sustainable level. The next decade is critical and will cost the industrialized world a fortune. The United States will fork over 3.5 trillion dollars over the next ten years, at a minimum. The world climate bill will be about 15-17 trillion dollars. Not one country has this kind of money to spend, unfortunately. Funding promises made since the Paris Climate Conference in 2015 have not been met. And, unfortunately, for every good, well thought out plan/project to improve the climate today and in the future, there are two new proposals which focus on the long term use of fossil fuels- oil, natural gas and even coal in many parts of the world and in particular, the United States. In the month of October 2023, ExxonMobil, and Chevron, two of this country's largest oil companies, purchased two smaller oil companies for 113 billion dollars. The announced plan is to further develop a number of oil fields in the country of Guyana, which are now producing 400,000 barrels of oil daily, but will increase that number to 1,200,000 barrels a day by 2027. Projects like this are announced daily across the globe. And there is a disturbing trend "Right now" in many countries to scale back on climate improvement projects that had been previously approved for funding. A recent and alarming announcement occurred in British Columbia where the regional government announced that it was canceling eighteen billion dollars' worth of climate improvement projects that had been approved. Reasons: Inflation, high interest costs and supply chain issues. This in an area of Canada which was devastated this past summer by raging, out of control firestorms that destroyed everything in its path for months.

On November 3, 2023, a total of five renewable energy windmill projects in New Jersey, Massachusetts, and Rhode Island were abruptly canceled by energy firms Orsted, British Petroleum and Equinor. Reasons: Inflation, high interest costs and supply chain issues. Billions of dollars have been lost in the process. In the State of New York, a number of windmill projects are in doubt. Energy investment exchanges are losing a fortune. Energy companies are reeling. At the same time, hundreds of billions of dollars are being invested in a variety of climate saving projects all over the world.

In terms of the environment, in what direction are we really going? This is a madness that will result in the waste of trillions of investment dollars by the industrialized world which, now, is not willing or ready to take the definitive actions it needs to take on a sustained basis. Certainly, approving fossil fuel projects that will ensure the utilization of oil and gas and even coal for the next one hundred years spells disaster for all of us. The evidence to prove this is irrefutable. In this country "Right now," coal is making a comeback for God's sake, thanks to the war in Ukraine.

War

Nothing is said in the media, the press, about what this country is doing in case of a Chinese invasion of Taiwan. I can assure you that there is at least one Operations Plan (OPLAN) somewhere in the Pentagon that outlines the force structure that would respond to such an invasion. In my military career, I worked on the medical support that would be needed in that type of OPLAN. From the OPLAN would come the Operations Order (OPORD) which would be the guide to defend Taiwan at a minimum.

A lot is currently being said in the media about Ukraine and Israel conflicts with Israel getting the most coverage and rightly so since the Ukraine war is in a stalemate and will remain so as the winter sets in on the European continent.

Israel is following its game plan for the absolute destruction of Hamas and, hopefully, Hezbollah down the road, despite huge worldwide protests by pro-Palestinian supporters. These protests, which get maximum coverage by this country's liberal press, do nothing more than encourage Israel to keep going and that is exactly what they are doing. Hamas will be wiped out in the short term.

What happens to Gaza is another story. What happens to the Palestinians, all two million of them, is another story. The deaths so far of 25,000 Palestinians is a human tragedy and the deaths of 1,200 Jews on October 7 is a human tragedy. The deaths of Jewish military are a human tragedy. The death of Hamas terrorists is a win for good over absolute evil. War is a human tragedy.

The United States must support Israel, Ukraine, and Taiwan against the evil out there. The cost of doing so is immense. Financial support for Ukraine will dwindle under Trump, will not under Biden and would not under Manchin. Troop involvement will not happen in Israel unless Iran enters the fray. Troop involvement in Ukraine will not happen unless Putin does something stupid like invade the country of Georgia or use a tactical nuclear weapon in Ukraine. The biggest challenge, if it develops, is China's final decision over Taiwan. The meeting between Biden and China's President Xi Jinping in California on November 16th may serve to improve relations between the two countries but it does not look like the two leaders had much of a discussion about Taiwan. They did reach consensus on the fentanyl issue, which is a good thing because China supplies Mexico with most of the chemicals needed to produce fentanyl. China would be smart to crack down on the production of these chemicals; otherwise, the new president might develop a different attitude on how to deal with China.

So, the issues surrounding our involvement in war relate directly to how much money we are willing to spend supporting the three scenarios mentioned, and all the other possible conflicts out there, which could explode at any time. Our funding for military support, at all levels, is limited when you consider all the other financial demands on the federal government. This includes the issues covered in this book but there are many other issues that require federal intervention and dollars. Quite frankly, I do not know how much longer this can go on. Debt is a terrible cancer for this country and its people.

One final thought on "War." What position has the United Nations taken on the Israeli/Hamas war? This is important because it seems that some countries are looking to the UN to get involved and solve the problem. First, the United States pays for one-fifth of the UN's annual budget, twelve billion out of sixty billion dollars. Biden restored the cuts Trump made when he was President. Trump thought the UN was corrupt (and it is) and this country was being unduly criticized for its position on immigration, Russian aggression, climate issues, and corruption in the organization itself. The UN has refused to label Hamas a terrorist organization. The UN Secretary General did condemn the Hamas invasion of Israel on October 7th, but he also accused Israel of committing war crimes after it entered Gaza. In addition, the United Nations Relief and Work Agency (UNRWA) advocates for Gaza by funding and providing school materials to Palestinian children that teach them to kill Jews. Maps in these teaching materials do not depict Israel as a country. Another reason Trump would not pay up. President Biden renewed UNRWA funding when he became president. The U.S. pays 330 million dollars annually to fund UNRWA activities. This funding was suspended on February 1, 2024, when it was discovered that numerous UNRWA employees participated in the October 7th invasion against Israel. Several U.N. member countries have also suspended funding.

(This is just another damning thing that the Biden Progressives do despite knowing full well that UNRWA practices antisemitism as part of its core philosophy. Trump also knew this and cut-off funding. Trump also knew that many U. N. member countries had not paid their dues in years. If Trump is elected, I would not be surprised if he cuts off funding again. We currently fund an organization that hates Jews to the tune of hundreds of millions of dollars a year, money that we must borrow! Pathetic. MLR)

Another final thought. I worry about our ability to supply our armed forces, including our Army Reserve and National Guard, with the equipment and armaments they will need for future operations. We are supplying Ukraine and Israel with weapons systems, ammunition, tanks, and other military vehicles produced in our factories and sending huge quantities of stockpiled everything to the point where we have little if anything left for our own force structure. Progressives will do this. They did it in Afghanistan when we pulled out of there in 2021. We left behind an estimated twelve billion dollars in equipment and weapons systems for the Taliban to use and resell on the black market.

The Economy

Bidenomics is a joke. It has been marked by stubborn inflation and high interest rates on everything, higher borrowing costs, and record consumer credit card debt. Most want –to-be home buyers are locked out of the real estate market because of the high cost of real estate. People are spending money they do not have (credit card debt is skyrocketing) and people who want to rent an apartment are looking at ever increasing rental costs across the country. This is not a good news scenario by any means. The challenge here is for the American voter to decide if this issue alone really favors Biden or someone else. This is where a third-party candidate can prevail for the first time ever in a presidential race. It will not be a Kennedy or a Stein, but it could be a legitimate, well-funded third-party candidate like Joe Manchin and his vice-presidential running mate, Condoleezza Rice, representing the No Labels Party or whatever it is called early next year when they announce. Or how about a Haley-Manchin ticket or a Manchin-Haley ticket or a DeSantis-Haley ticket or a Haley-DeSantis ticket or a Manchin-DeSantis ticket or a DeSantis-Manchin ticket. Getting Condoleezza Rice on a ticket in any capacity is my hope but I must admit it is a long, long shot. How about a Haley-Rice ticket?

"Right now," the Biden Administration will do nothing to change the immigration problem in the next twelve months. It is clear to me that the Biden Administration will propose no major legislation that will impact the drug scourge this country is facing. The recent major drug busts that have taken place across the country are good news, but it is not enough. It is clear to me that the Biden Administration will do nothing to reduce the national debt and stop borrowing endless amounts of money in the next twelve months to pay bills. It is clear to me that the Biden Administration will need at least another ten years of criminal prosecutions to deal with the thousands of fraud arrests that have occurred in the last two years from the theft of at least two trillion dollars from the progressive giveaway legislation. It is clear to me that we will continue to get mixed results from the Biden Administration's completely screwed up policy on climate control. For every policy decision to limit the use of fossil fuels, there are two policy decisions that prolong the use of fossil fuels for the next one hundred years, wasting trillions of taxpayer dollars.

I am supportive of Biden's war policies. We have no choice but to support Ukraine, Israel, and Taiwan when that specific situation unfolds. It could be a world ending situation. We are living in the most dangerous times since the Cold War when a couple of nuclear bombs could have ended it all. Some of you certainly, remember the Cuban Missile Crisis?

God Bless America!

Chapter 10: Afterword

My hope with this book was to present a coherent chapter by chapter position for each of the major issues written about. The fact is I have had great difficulty maintaining a semblance of coherence on these issues. Daily, the issues covered, that I believe are so important to all of us, have proven so volatile that new developments occur hourly, which proves how relevant they are to our very survival. It is a period of chaos, disunity, and tragedy. Effective today, December 6, 2023, the day before Pearl Harbor Day, I have decided to post a daily dairy, when appropriate, of all significant events that take place related to any of the eight chapters in this book, until it goes to print. Of course, I may have an opinion thrown in there once in a while and I know there will be disagreements on just what is relevant and worthy of update.

Chapter 1 - The U.S. Political System

On December 6, 2023, all hell broke loose for three presidents of prestigious universities at a congressional hearing on anti-Semitic demonstrations on university and college campuses across the country. President Liz Magill of the University of Pennsylvania, President Claudine Gay of Harvard University, and President Sally Kornbluth of the Massachusetts Institute of Technology (MIT), were asked the same question by Rep. Elise Stefanik (R-NY), a Harvard graduate: "Does calling for the genocide of Jews violate your institution's code of conduct or rules regarding bullying and harassment?" All three individuals failed to definitively answer the question, two of them calling it a question of context and one saying individuals had to be the target. The question of course related to the October 7th, 2023, Hamas surprise invasion of southern Israel which resulted in the massacre of 1,200 Jewish men, women, and children and several hundred Jewish hostages taken to Gaza by these animals. And, almost immediately, anti-Semitic protests sprang up at U.S. universities and colleges, the focus being on the Palestinians killed by invading Israeli Defense Force (IDF) forces.

(Can you imagine? This is what you get today from the far-left Progressives in charge of elite institutions. The attitude filters down to the entire scholastic community, as it certainly had on these three campuses. As a result, many powerful people are calling for these three leaders to resign, which I hope happens quickly. Donors are pulling their donations in the millions of dollars. It is not just in government that this country must get back to the middle of the social/political spectrum. Nothing wrong with being a Centrist. MLR)

On Saturday, December 9, 2023, Liz Magill, UPENN president, resigned.

(This was not a surprise to anyone. Her appearance before a House sub-committee was a complete disaster. Scott Bok, chairman of the Board of Trustees, also resigned. This same weekend, many of the faculty at Harvard, some seven hundred strong, sent a letter to the Harvard Board of Overseers requesting it not fire Claudine Gay. It would not surprise me if the letter is persuasive. It does go to demonstrate how far left and how far gone from reality some people can go off the political/social spectrum. In this country "Right now," we must get back to the middle of this spectrum because what we have now is an abomination. MLR)

(On December 11, 2023, The Harvard Corporation and the Harvard Board of Overseers, the school's two governing bodies, voted to allow Harvard University President, Dr. Claudine Gay, to

remain in her position. This is a disgrace and I for one do not believe this issue is resolved, based on the swift reaction from members of Congress. My feeling is that Harvard University will lose millions of federal research and education dollars in the short term. She will resign in the end, maybe not for her anti-Semitic position, but for something else. MLR)**

On January 3, 2024, Dr. Claudine Gay resigned as President of Harvard University. At the same time, she was reinstated as a professor at the school at an annual salary of 900,000 dollars plus benefits.

(This is not hard to believe considering that very few people at Harvard believe she did anything wrong, but it is hard to accept. In any event, she is no longer president and that is a good thing. MLR)

Speaking once again of Harvard University, the New York Post published an astonishing article December 24, 2023, on federal monies paid to elite universities across the country. Harvard was used as a very appropriate example of the corrupt system that receives billions of dollars year after year after year from a variety of sources.

In 2023, here is what Harvard received: 676 million dollars from the federal government; twenty-five million dollars in "COVID Rescue" funds from the feds; 349 million from the state of Massachusetts; 2,461 million dollars in investment funds; (donations?) and untold millions from Pell grants and student loans. On top of this Harvard enjoys tax free status and pays a paltry 1.4% of all income while business pays 37%. It pays nothing on capital gains on share or bond sales; it pays nothing on its dividend income; and it pays no corporate taxes. The going rate of taxation for business on most of these categories is 37%.

(This is a pretty good deal for a university that has an endowment fund worth 51 billion dollars at this writing. I wondered how Harvard could pay Dr. Gay, now a professor, a salary of nine hundred thousand dollars a year plus great benefits I would assume.

Now I know. Something must give here. This is only one university. What about Yale, Brown, Dartmouth, MIT and so many other universities in the United States. I think this government should force these institutions to spend some of their endowments and rely a lot less on the government's dole. The U. S. national debt just went over 34+ trillion dollars. I also do not understand this tax-free status. Seems inappropriate now. The day of reckoning for these elite schools may be approaching. If Trump wins the 2024 election, he will be hard pressed by Congress, no matter who controls it, to put a sledgehammer to the economic policies currently in place, policies which favor these elite schools now experiencing daily antisemitism demonstrations on campuses across the country. There is growing sentiment among Democrats and Republicans in the Congress to change the financial policies now in effect, policies which suck the wind out of the federal treasury. Certainly, any foreign students found on any campus yelling "from the river to the sea" should immediately be sent home. Graduates who demonstrate should be flagged by the major investment and banking corporations that look at Harvard and Yale graduates, et al and refuse to interview them and that is in fact happening. With regards to the financial changes, it is an amazingly simple solution. These schools should pay the going tax rates if they are receiving federal dollars, period. That rate would be 37%, period. If the finances get a little tight, lower faculty salaries by 15%, perhaps a little more. At 15%, Dr. Gay's salary of nine hundred thousand dollars would be reduced to 765 thousand dollars annually. I could live on that. That is still a weekly salary of 14,500 dollars (approximately). Or take a billion or two from the endowment. For Harvard, that would still leave forty-nine billion dollars in the bank, growing every day with interest. This is another case where I decided to place this issue under Chapter 1, "U.S. Political System". It could have been placed under the "Economy" chapter or even the "War" chapter. So often you discover that these chapters are interrelated. MLR)

Another glaring example of elite universities out of control, an article in the Washington Post released on January 25, 2024, described an agreement in a Washington DC court involving half a dozen of the nation's top universities who conspired to limit financial aid for admitted students, mostly from working and middle-class families. They agreed to pay 104.5 million dollars to settle their involvement in the matter. The initial suit, filed by eight impacted students, involved nineteen elite schools, including most members of the Ivy League (Harvard was not mentioned). The students claimed the schools conspired to "fix "the allocation of funds to ensure that the schools paid less than would have been required if the conspiracy did not exist. A total of eight schools have settled. A total of two hundred thousand students were impacted by the practice which went on for twenty years. The schools which settled: Duke University, Columbia University, Yale University, Emory University, Brown University, Georgetown University, and the California Institute of Technology. The remaining schools are still in negotiations. The money will go into a pool and will eventually be distributed to the impacted students.

(Once again, nobody gets indicted, nobody goes to jail, and nobody loses a job. The post-secondary education hierarchy in this country seems to be totally in charge of itself. They are the elephants in the room. They can do what they want, and the federal government seems powerless to act. It is the courts that seem to be the leverage from the cases I researched. This reality, if it is accurate, did not develop overnight and it will take years for reform to take place. In the meantime, this is a situation that can be managed if this outcome is taken seriously by the academic community. What do you think? MLR).

Today, 12/7/23, U.S. Representative Kevin McCarthy (D-CA), former speaker of the House, the first speaker to be ousted from this post, announced his resignation from the House at the end of the year. This resignation reduces the Republican majority in the House from three to two seats. A special election will be held in California in the next four months to choose a replacement. Also today, Representative Jamaal Bowman of New York was censured by the House of Representatives for pulling a fire alarm in the House in October to delay a crucial vote on the first Continuing Resolution, which would have caused a government shutdown. Bowman has already pled guilty and paid a fine. He is a far-left leaning socialist Democrat, who has condemned Israel and demanded a permanent cease fire in that conflict.

(Fortunately, Bowman will be challenged in the New York Democratic primary next year by George Latimer, a popular Westchester County, New York executive. Many key New York Democrats are urging Bowman to step down. He should. America has had enough of these radical left wings idiots who engage in outrageous behavior, and nothing happens. Bowman is just one of a dozen hard left and hard right incumbents that must go if this country has any chance of balancing itself out. MLR)

On this day, former temporary House Speaker, Rep. Patrick McHenry (R-NC), announced that he will not seek re-election next year. This is significant because he is just one of a dozen incumbents who have announced they will not run again. The problem is that the people leaving are mostly moderates who came to Washington to do good; instead, they must sit there and put up with all the bullshit from the hard left, hard right idiots that have brought government to a standstill. Many leaving have simply had enough. And there will be more.

On December 6, 2023, another national televised Republican debate took place. There were four individuals present, Chris Christie, Ron DeSantis, Nikki Haley, and Vivek Ramaswamy. After the affair was over, it was pretty clear to me that soon there will be two candidates left - DeSantis and Haley. Ramaswamy is an insulting, demeaning human being who is unfit for political office. Christie is not convincing enough but I do not dislike him or his politics. I am drawn to Haley.

(The more I see her in action the more I like her. I do believe that a Haley-Rice ticket would work for this country. MLR)

A potentially devastating event occurred in the U. S. House of Representatives on December 13, 2023: a presidential impeachment inquiry resolution, put forth by Representative Marjorie Greene (R-GA-14) on January 21, 2021, was passed along party lines- Republican 221, Democratic 212. If the eventual vote to impeach passes in the House, President Joe Biden will stand impeached and will be tried in the U.S. Senate on charges of abuse of power by enabling bribery (around his son Hunter's influence pedaling when Biden was vice-president in the Obama administration) and other high crimes and misdemeanors. The inquiry will be conducted by the House Judiciary, Oversight, and Ways and Means Committees.

Democrats are calling this maneuver a sick political stunt and cite Donald Trump's involvement in the process. Republicans counter that they have evidence that over twenty-two million dollars was distributed to many members of the Biden family during that period and there is strong evidence that Hunter routinely used his father's name as leverage when dealing with his Chinese and Ukrainian business partners, who provided most of the funds in question.

Congressional investigators have almost forty thousand pages of subpoenaed bank records from numerous accounts and testimony from key witnesses that paint a dark picture for the Biden family during a critical time less than a year before the next national election. The liberal press has downplayed the entire investigation but has indicated there are certainly some concerns about ethical lapses by the Biden family but no criminal evidence. Republicans claim that the proof is there but stonewalling by key Democratic figures in the investigation have forced the impeachment inquiry forward to subpoena reluctant witnesses under threat of contempt if they refuse to answer questions or provide documents to the committees. This process will be hard for the average American to tolerate because the average American is tired of all this crap, has been for some time.

If there is a trial, the Senate would need sixty-seven votes to convict, which will be next to impossible because the Senate is controlled by Democrats.

(The House vote will be close, but I think Biden will be impeached. It will be like the two Trump impeachment votes that took place during his administration. In the Senate, Biden will be exonerated just like Trump was twice in the Senate. At that time, the House was in control of Democrats and the Senate was in control of Republicans. This is what politics in this country has come to. My concern is that things are so crazy "Right now" Biden just might be found guilty in the Senate and get kicked out of office. One thing is certain, if Trump is elected in 2024, the next four years will look exactly like it is "Right now," tit for tat. Trump will go after every Democrat he can to get even for what he is going through "Right now" in criminal and civil courts all over the country. A key factor to consider is the Congress and who ends up controlling it after the 2024 election. Voting out the hard left-hard right idiots that have brought this country to a standstill is paramount and challengers to some of these idiots are emerging for future House and Senate races. We need a third-party slate to be announced soon. When that happens, the voters in this country must stand up and do what is right. We cannot survive an election that pits Biden against Trump nor can we survive an election where many of these idiots are re-elected. MLR)

(On January 14, 2024, Senator Joe Manchin announced that he is still considering a third party run for President of the United States, probably under the "No Labels Party" banner. The problem is that nobody has heard from the no labels people in months. And the fact that they have cancelled their proposed national convention in April 2024, does not exactly instill confidence. The last word from them several weeks ago was that they would make a final determination on a presidential challenge by mid-March 2024. I think an announcement in March is too late. MLR)

On Friday, February 16, 2024, Senator Joe Manchin announced that he will not be running for president in the 2024 election race. "I will not be seeking a third-party run" he said at a speech at West Virginia University. He had been considered one of the top candidates to head a third-party ticket sponsored by the No Labels movement based in Washington DC.

(For me, this was very disappointing news. No Labels must act soon, or it will be a Biden-Trump race straight to hell. MLR)

On December 12, 2023, the Wall Street Journal published an article highlighting that the state of Colorado's Supreme Court voted 4-3 to disqualify Donald Trump from being on the Colorado state presidential ballot because of insurrection under Section 3 of the 14th Amendment to the U.S. Constitution. The position of the court was that Trump was the catalyst for the attack on the U. S. Capitol based on the speech he gave just blocks from the Capitol a short time before the vicious attack. Trump's lawyers immediately appealed the case to the U. S. Appeals Court and from there to the Supreme Court no matter what the Appeals Court rules. In early January 2024, the state of Maine Supreme Court also ruled that Trump could not be on the state's presidential ballot for the same reason. The Maine Supreme Court ruled that its case will remain in the state court until a decision is made on the Colorado case.

To date, thirty-five states have petitioned their state courts to bar Trump from its state presidential ballot for insurrection.

The Supreme Court in Michigan has ruled in Trump's favor and no appeal has been indicated by the state of Michigan presently. The Illinois Board of Electors recently ruled that Trump will remain on that state's presidential ballot.

(Trump will appeal any decision that does not go his way. Money is no object, and these appeals will take time. Even if Colorado wins its case, Trump's name will most likely remain on the ballot if too much time lapses. People will vote for him, but the votes will not count, which is another testament to how screwed up everything is in this country. "Right now," we are upside down. MLR)

As of Saturday, February 17, 2024, the U. S. Supreme Court has heard the Trump appeal and will offer a decision soon. The general reaction by left-wing and right-wing experts is that Trump will win easily, based on the questions from the nine justices. Most commentators believe that the decision will be unanimously in Trump's favor.

(Sadly, I must agree. The justices, one and all, seemed to think that the states have no business to impede a candidate running for federal office even though the Oregon lawyers made a strong case alleging that Trump had violated the 14th Amendment to the U. S. Constitution by his raucous speech near the U. S. Capitol on January 6, 2021, which they contended ultimately lead to the infamous assault. Trump was still President of the United States at the time. MLR)

On March 3, 2024, the U.S. Supreme Court ruled unanimously that Trump will remain on the Oregon ballot. That ends the question of immunity on the minds of the other thirty-five states who wanted Trump off their election ballots.

(This ruling is a big victory for Trump, and it comes one day before Super Tuesday! Most people who cared knew this would be the outcome. Trump, standing between a bunch of American flags, thanked the Supreme Court on national news. He was very subdued, almost humble. Of course, just a few hours before, when Trump learned that Nikki Haley had won the Washington, DC primary, he called her a loser. Not very nice. He will have a very different attitude when this same Supreme Court rules against him on the immunity issue in the near future. MLR)

On February 25, 2024, Trump won the South Carolina primary over Nikki Haley by sixty points, a huge victory. He won all twenty-nine delegates. South Carolina is Haley's home state. She was a popular governor there. Haley vowed to continue, and she has.

Several other Republican primaries have concluded and the results in Iowa and New Hampshire favored Donald Trump by wide margins. On January 15, 2024, Trump cruised to victory in Iowa with 51% of the vote, DeSantis came in second with 21%, and Haley a close third with 18.9%. This forced Vivek Ramaswamy to drop out of the race. Ramaswamy immediately threw his support to Trump. In the New Hampshire primary, Trump got more than 50% of the 300,000 +votes cast, a new record for New Hampshire voters. The day before the primary, DeSantis dropped out and immediately threw his support to Trump. On January 22, 2024, Trump won by eight points over Haley, who simply congratulated Trump and moved onto South Carolina.

(The next primary is in Nevada, where Trump has a demanding lead and will win that primary by a landslide. Haley is counting on a win in South Carolina, her home-state where she was once the governor. The problem is that the current Republican leadership in that state, from the governor on down, have all endorsed Trump, who has a double-digit commanding lead there. It does not look good for Haley or this country. Trump was in court when he was not in

Iowa or New Hampshire and his margins keep increasing! It is truly overwhelming. I believe Haley will drop out after the South Carolina primary. I really hope she wins there. In Iowa, Republican voters overwhelmingly (88%) want a change in the way this country is run; immigration is a major concern (75%); and 71% favor the completion of a southern border wall. MLR)

On January 26, 2024, a New York court hit Donald Trump with an 88.3-million-dollar defamation judgment in favor of E. Jean Carroll, who had previously been awarded five million dollars in a civil suit in that same court in May of 2023 against the same guy. She was awarded eighteen million dollars for the personal harm she experienced and sixty-five million dollars for punitive damages. Trump and his lawyers have promised to appeal this decision as well. The appeals will take forever as they always do in our court system and will not be decided until well after the 2024 election.

(Donald Trump managed to turn a 5-million-dollar loss into an 88.3-million-dollar loss all because of his big mouth and still, a lot of people in this country want him to be our next president. This is just one of several reasons why this country is "upside down." Unfortunately, many anti-Trump voters look at the alternative- Biden- Harris- and they realize they have a decision to make, not to vote at all or vote for one of the alternatives, Kennedy, or Stein, which for most voters is not an alternative at all. Rather than not vote, many will vote for Trump with great reservations. For me, I am going to vote for somebody who is running. If No Labels decides not to put forward a slate, I will not vote for "Donald Duck" or a Kennedy or a Stein. I will vote for Donald Trump because this country has had enough, I have had enough, of these fanatic progressive left-wing Democrats. I will vote for a No Labels slate if one is presented. However, time is running out for that party to announce. MLR)

On Tuesday, February 6, 2024, a three-judge panel on the Washington, DC U.S. Circuit Court of Appeals, ruled unanimously that Donald Trump is not immune from prosecution, not above the law, for actions he took while President of the United States. The court ruled that he can stand trial because he illegally plotted to overthrow the 2020 presidential election. The judges indicated in their decision that Trump should appeal the case directly to the Supreme Court. In return the judges ruled that his criminal case would be stayed until the Supreme Court rendered a final decision.

This decision is a huge defeat for Trump and a huge victory for Special Counsel Jack Smith, who is prosecuting the criminal case against Trump in Washington, DC Federal Court. If Trump appeals directly to the Supreme Court and the Court refuses to hear the case, it will go back to the federal district court in two-three weeks. If the Supreme Court hears the case, the process will take months and a final decision would not be handed down until the June-July timeframe. If the Supreme Court rules against Trump, the case returns to the district court for trial, which had originally been scheduled to start in March but the presiding Judge Tanya S. Chutkan, cancelled that proceeding, based on an appeal going forward. If a trial becomes a reality the feeling is that it must start in the fall to be decided by the November election. Otherwise, a trial would be held after the election sometime in early 2025. In that scenario, if Trump wins the election, he could simply ask the Department of Justice (DOJ) to dismiss the case. If he is found guilty, he could simply pardon himself.

(Trump will most certainly appeal. If he appeals to the full Circuit Court of Appeals and that ends up going to the Supreme Court, this case goes well into 2025 before it is resolved. I give a lot of credit to the 3-judge panel for attempting to legitimately speed up this case in the hope that it could be decided by the November election. A lot is riding on this process. Not only Trump could suffer from court/case fatigue, but many Republican candidates for office

(Trump supporters) throughout the country could feel the change of attitude I believe many Republican voters will have if Trump must go to trial. MLR)

On February 29, 2024, the U. S. Supreme Court agreed to hear the Immunity case, which will delay the criminal trial indefinitely. Arguments will take place the week of April 22nd. The Supreme Court's calendar ends at the end of June 2024. On the same day, the New York State Appeals Court rejected Trump's bid to pause action on the recent $450 million-dollar civil judgment that was assessed in that state's court system.

(For Trump, his delaying tactics on all his civil and criminal cases works in some instances and not in others. For him timing is everything. On the immunity case, it is quite possible he will not go to trial until after the November election. On the civil judgment, he does not have the finances to pay-up. His lawyers asked the court for a break, and they did not get one. This case should prove very interesting as it comes to closure. It would be something out of a mystical, magical playbook if Trump had to ask a criminal court for a continuance so he could attend his own presidential swearing-in. MLR)

On March 9, 2024, Trump's lawyers announced that they have succeeded in posting a 91.6 million dollars bond in the E. Jean Carroll case, which will allow them to immediately appeal the decision to the US Court of Appeals for the 2nd Circuit Court. The bond was guaranteed by Chubbs, one of the largest insurance companies in the country.

(This bond should quiet the Progressives who have always claimed that Trump is not particularly wealthy. The terms of the deal were not made public but most experts in the field believe that Trump had to pay a premium of 1-3% of the judgment. At 1%, that would be 880 thousand dollars; at 3%, the fee would be 2, 640 thousand dollars. He would also have to pledge collateral to cover

the remaining judgment. The interest was added to the judgment amount, which brought the bond total to 91.6 million dollars. In the initial 5-million-dollar judgment for Carroll, Trump posted 5.6 million dollars in cash with the court and immediately filed his appeal in that case. In his fraud case, a separate case decided recently, the court hit him with a civil penalty of 456 million dollars. His lawyers offered to post a 100-million-dollar bond to appeal but the presiding judge turned it down. He did allow a hearing before a 5-judge panel without a posted bond. If the judge's rule against Trump he will have to post a bond or the amount of the judgment by March 25, 2024. If he fails to do that, the Attorney General of the state of New York could move to collect the judgment. It is worth stating here that the date of Trump's criminal trial in New York is also March 25, 2024. It just keeps getting worse for the guy, but it just keeps getting better in his run for the presidency. It really is the most bizarre thing, completely "Upside down." MLR)

You lose one, you lose two, maybe three. Also on Tuesday, the Republican majority in the U. S. House of Representatives voted to impeach Homeland Security Secretary Alejandro Mayorkas but the action fell short as four Republicans switched their votes at the last second. The Republicans accused Mayorkas of lying to Congress and refusing to comply with immigration law. Prior to the vote, all 216 GOP lawmakers had voted to move the motion forward. The final vote was 216-214 to defeat the motion.

(You would think that should be the end of it. After the vote, several Republicans indicated they will attempt to have another vote in a week or two when they are sure all Republicans will be present for the vote. Mayorkas is simply following his boss's orders. He answers directly to Joe Biden. Going after Mayorkas again is akin to double jeopardy in a court trial. If there is a second vote, I hope it fails. I am no fan of this guy trust me. He has lost control of the border situation. However, the man is now being harassed. In better times, when politicians were getting along and could communicate and negotiate, this kind of travesty would not happen. MLR)

(On Wednesday, February 14, 2024, the House of Representatives, by one vote, voted to impeach Alejandro Mayorkas. The motion will now move to the U. S. Senate for an impeachment trial. This is beyond disgusting and a waste of time and a huge amount of money. The U. S. Senate is controlled by Democrats. Mayorkas is a Democrat who has strong support of Democratic Senators. He will not be convicted, and Republicans know this full well. MLR)

Again, on February 6, 2024, the Senate's multi-billion-dollar border bill to fund Ukraine and Israel and establish broad new policies for the southern border, went up in smoke as Senate Republicans by one vote defeated the measure after Donald Trump expressed his displeasure. House Speaker Mike Johnson, a disciple of Trump, had said that the bill as negotiated was "dead on arrival" if it is sent to the House of Representatives for consideration. The bill, which was the result of intense and daily negotiations between Senate Republicans and Democrats, provided the strongest border policy revisions ever proposed in Congress. It also provides the much need foreign aid to Israel and Ukraine. Among other things, the bill provided sixty billion dollars for border security, 650 million dollars for border wall construction, and Title 42 authority to shut down all crossings when migrant encounters exceed five thousand immigrants over a one-week period and a tightening of the asylum process. Now that the bill is dead in the water, there is no money for anybody or anything. As a result, the Senate is now constructing a stand-alone foreign aid bill for Israel and Ukraine.

(It just gets worse and worse. It is now the month of February 2024, five months into FY 2023-2024, and we still do not have a federal budget. Nobody in Congress is even talking about the current

Continuing Resolution which is our federal budget, and which expires in just a couple of weeks. This is all happening because of the hard right elements in Congress. This has the handprint of Donald Trump all over everything. With each passing day, it gets worse for the average American. We are getting closer and closer to financial Armageddon, war is closing in on us, like it or not and we continue to borrow billions of dollars every day non-stop at the federal level. I have not seen it in such a state of deep paralysis in national government in my 79 years on this earth. MLR)

Despite the initial vote-down on this bill, the U. S. Senate came right back with a new foreign aid bill without any border provisions on February 12, 2024. This time around eighteen Republicans voted for the passed bill, giving Donald Trump and his right-wing Republicans in the Senate and the House, a huge defeat. The bill carries a price tag in the range of ninety-five billion dollars-60.1 billion dollars to Ukraine and 14.1 billion dollars to Israel. The Republican Speaker of the House, Mike Johnson, declared this bill "Dead on Arrival" as well.

(This aid money is desperately needed by Ukraine. The land battle there is going downhill, ammunition is short, money is tight and new recruits are getting harder to recruit. Israel will not turn the money down because it is becoming very clear that Israel will be in Gaza for a long time and Hezbollah in Lebanon will have to be dealt with in a big way sooner than later. The U. S. House will vote this bill down as well. They are not budging on their demand for major immigration reform before any aid goes to a foreign country. This issue will hang in the air for at least two more weeks because the Congress just went on a two-week break. I am hoping this Republican break-out vote to pass this bill is a growing trend in Congress. There are serious challenges approaching-the FY 2024 budget, a Continuing Resolution if no budget, foreign aid still, budget cuts and border issues that have nothing to do with money.

If this is not a trend, there is going to be hell to pay in this country. MLR)

A special counsel report released on Thursday, February 8, 2024, found ample evidence that President Joe Biden did mishandle classified information while he was vice-president during the Obama administration. Special Counsel Robert Hur indicated in the report that criminal charges were not warranted because the government would not be able to prove Biden's intent beyond a reasonable doubt. This situation, according to Hur, was made more difficult because of Biden's advanced age, memory loss and inability to recall facts.

(This report ends, once and for all, any chance of criminal charges against Biden. Of all his problems, this one was the least of his worries all along. MLR)

On February 15, 2024, Judge Juan Manuel Merchant of the New York Federal District Court ruled that Trump's criminal case will go forward on March 25, 2024. This decision means that this case, involving the alleged payment of hush money to women he had affairs with while married to his current wife, will be the first of four to go to trial. The allegations go all the way back to Trump's race for the presidency in 2016, some eight years ago. This case is considered by many to be the weakest of the four cases he faces.

(Weak case or not, it puts tremendous pressure on Trump to be in potentially many places at once and not for campaigning for the presidency. How he will survive the next eight or nine months is beyond me. The fact is he tried to hide these payments through his political apparatus and failed miserably when the feds arrested his attorney who had provided the payments on Trump's approval. The attorney, Michael Cohen ratted out Trump in a heartbeat but still got jail time and Trump could too. MLR)

In an unrelated but very important civil case involving Trump and two members of his family, a Manhattan Supreme Court Justice, Arthur Engoron, fined Trump 355 million dollars and banned him from serving as an officer or director of any company in New York for three years. He also fined Trump's two sons four million dollars each and banned them from office holding for two years. There were a number of additional rulings which required Trump to hire independent financial and accounting experts who will execute compliance standards at his various New York based companies. If Trump appeals, which he has said he will, he must, by New York state law arrange a security bond to cover the 355-million-dollar penalty plus a 9% interest rate, before he appeals. Many people believe he will not be able to do that. The cost of a bond could go as high as seventy million dollars. One ruling in Trump's favor- the judge rescinded a previous order to dissolve his New York based businesses.

(I am praying that this historic civil decision begins to convince Trump supporters that he is not worth it. Trump will be found guilty in Georgia, but that trial will not happen until sometime in early 2025, especially when you consider the crap going on right now with Fulton County District Attorney Fani Willis and her special prosecutor boyfriend, Nathan Wade. The worst-case scenario is that Trump and his eighteen co-defendants are let go because of these two lovebirds' antics. What I hope happens is that the lawyers are dismissed, and a new prosecuting team is named. That will mean a big delay in any trial. I do strongly believe that Trump goes to jail if found guilty. This is a state case which Trump cannot touch with a pardon. The other federal cases are serious in nature and any publicity that develops over the next 6 months could change a lot of minds. MLR)

On March 2, 2024, Trump won caucuses in Missouri and Idaho and all the delegates in Michigan. The current count now stands 244-24 in

Trump's favor, with a grand total of 1,215 delegate votes needed to secure the Republican presidential nomination.

(Super Tuesday on March 5 should seal Nikki Haley's fate. What happened in Missouri, Idaho and Michigan did not surprise anyone. Nevertheless, the fact that over 100,000 thousand Michigan Democrats voted as uncommitted could spell big trouble for Biden, who is believed by more and more Democrats to be too old and too mentally and physically challenged to do the job. In Michigan, many people who voted "uncommitted" said in exit polls that they voted that way because of Biden's support for Israel in that country's current conflict in Gaza. Recent national polls have Trump clearly ahead of Biden in the presidential race. It is early. MLR)

"Super Tuesday," March 5, 2024, was a monumental victory for Donald Trump. He won 14 of 15 states involved including every important swing state - Michigan, Pennsylvania, Georgia, Wisconsin, and Arizona. The Senate Majority leader, Mitch McConnell, immediately endorsed Trump and called for party unity on his run. Haley, as expected, dropped out of the race without endorsing Trump. President Biden won his primaries going away. As many feared, the race is now Biden vs. Trump.

(After it was all over, Trump congratulated Haley on a good run and then called her a loser. When he got around to Biden, he mocked him by stuttering during his speech and people laughed and applauded. God help us please. MLR)

I am hoping this is an announcement that will change everything for this country as it approaches the November election. "No Labels" announced that it will run a slate of candidates for the election. On March 8, 2024, Mike Rawlins, the convention chairman, told reporters that the eight hundred No Label delegates from the fifty states had met on the issue of nominations and voted unanimously to support a presidential slate. The candidates will be announced shortly. Joe Manchin will not be considered as he recently indicated he was retiring from politics. There is speculation that Chris Christie from New Jersey or possibly Nikki Haley may be named. The initial goal, stated many months ago, was to develop a slate of centrists (moderate conservatives) including Democrats and Republicans.

(I am hopeful beyond words that this is all true. If it is true, a bi-partisan ticket will attract voters in numbers big enough to win the election. I understand third party candidates have not done well historically in a presidential election in this country. Forget Kennedy and Stein. Congratulate them for running but they have absolutely no impact. Once again, this is where the individual vote can make a big difference. I am eager to know who will be announced and I do not care. I will vote the "No Labels" ticket because a Biden or a Trump in the highest office in the land in 2025 for the next four years is untenable. MLR)

Chapter 2 - Immigration

On December 6, 2023, the United States set a one-day record with more than 12,000 migrants crossing over our southern border into this country. Ten thousand, two hundred crossed undocumented into the country between ports of entry. For the month of December 2023, a total of 249, 000 immigrants crossed into the United States.

(This cannot continue much longer. This country is maxed out in terms of capacity and cost. Now we are seeing middle class Chinese citizens showing up at the border offering huge sums of money to get them into the U.S. Please remember that a moderate presidential ticket will do much the same thing Trump is promising if elected. A moderate, bi-partisan ticket will shut down our borders and detain migrants for returning to their countries of origin. Trump will do a lot more because he is a violent guy who derives a lot of pleasure using power. He is a true egomaniac. MLR)

Michael L. Roeder

In Europe, during the month of December 2023, a number of countries tightened their immigration laws because of increasing numbers of immigrants seeking entry into countries like England, France, Germany, and the Netherlands. In England, a controversial policy has been approved for immigrants who are denied asylum. They will be deported to Rwanda in Africa where their cases will be heard. If they win, they remain in Rwanda. They cannot return to England. This is deterrence personified. England has already paid Rwanda over three hundred million dollars in their contract, and nobody has been deported yet. In France, the welcome mat has been pulled, undocumented immigrants are now being held and deported quickly. For those immigrants who manage to remain in France, they will now have limited access to welfare and citizenship. Also, immigrants must be able to speak French to get a residency permit and children born in France to foreign parents will no longer get French citizenship. In Germany there are plans to send some asylum seekers to Africa while their cases are adjudicated in Germany. Over one million asylum cases are pending in the German courts. In the Netherlands, a far-right anti-immigrant candidate for president won in a landslide. He had vowed to end the undocumented immigrant nightmare which has engulfed that country. Across Europe, the far-right political parties are gaining ground because the average European is fed up with the immigration issue.

(Undocumented immigration is not just an American problem. It is a worldwide phenomenon because the entire world is on the move. Millions of people, most of them poor, uneducated, unskilled, and hopeless, are heading somewhere, anywhere for a better life. In the United States, a country where the problem is completely out of control, Donald Trump is the one person who can and will change the formula if he is elected. MLR)

A January 25, 2024, article on Humanitarian Parole in the New York Times got me to wondering again about an issue that many people talk about in my circles:

"How many immigrants, legal and undocumented, are living in this country today?" This compelled me to investigate this issue again, even though I have written extensively about those numbers, primarily because nobody, including government experts, seem to really know. Here is my current estimate:

- Dreamers: children brought into the country illegally by their parents-1 million (estimate supported by government data.)

- Gotaways: undocumented immigrants who managed to get into this country without being detected- 1 million (estimate not supported by much of anything.)

- Humanitarian Parole: people without visas allowed to live and work in this country temporarily due to "urgent humanitarian needs"- 1.3 million. (Reliable statistic provided by federal government. Biden has let in this number in the last three years.)

- Visa overstays immigrants who visit but never return to their home country- 1.5 million (Who knows. Could be 750,000 or close to 1.5 million.) Undocumented immigrants in the country before Biden became president: twelve million (government estimate.)

- Immigrants allowed into this country at our borders by the Biden administration, mostly unvetted-3 million.

- The total is 19.8 million men, women, and children.

(Unvetted Immigrants let into this country now are not considered undocumented because they have made a claim for asylum and have been allowed into the country with a court date 3-5 years down the road, never to be seen again could be off by three million immigrants. MLR)

Speaking of humanitarian parole, on March 10, 2024, the New York Times did an expose (I call it that because who knew?) on humanitarian parole as used extensively by this administration. In the last 18 months, over 300, 000 immigrants exclusively from Cuba, Haiti, Nicaragua, and Venezuela have been flown into this country and given short term legal status and job permits under the guise of humanitarian parole. We will pay for the trip. The one positive feature of this program is that the immigrants must have a financial sponsor for the two years they are allowed to remain in this country. There is also a parole program exclusively for Ukrainian citizens. Recently, a federal judge ruled for the program after the states of Texas, Florida, Tennessee, and Arkansas sued the federal government on the grounds the program was still costing the states millions of dollars in education, housing and other costs not covered by sponsors.

(The overall numbers of immigrants are staggering and will continue to explode if Biden is re-elected in November. Trump will put a stop to all this overwhelming expense for sure. But so will "No Labels." Congress might do something but only if a lot of current extremists are voted out of office. We are entering a critical moment in this country's history. I am worried. MLR)

On January 31, 2024, in the failing city of New York, NY, several migrants viciously attacked and beat two New York police officers who were simply doing their jobs to maintain law and order in Times Square. Gangs have been forming in the city and they are increasingly causing crime on the streets with assaults, robberies, pickpocketing, and other thefts. As the two-officers attempted to break up a crowd of youths, all migrants, they were assaulted and overcome. One of the officers was repeatedly kicked in the head and had to be taken to a local hospital for treatment. Five individuals, all in their teens and early twenties and all un-vetted immigrants, were arrested and taken to court where they were released without bond on misdemeanor charges. Several of the arrestees, as they were leaving court, gleefully gave the reporters and others present the double-barreled middle finger, smiling and claiming they could not speak English. Two of the arrested had previous charges pending in the court system already. New York Governor Kathy Hochul wanted them deported because "they can't touch other people; they can't touch police officers."

(Well, they do in fact touch police officers, with their fists and boots. Even the liberal media thought this was an outrage. It is a grievous symptom of what is to come for this country. Serious offenses which turn out to be simple misdemeanor arrests, no bail, a court continuance which will never come to fruition in these cases because the perpetrators, using false names, managed the next day to get on a charity bus bound for California. "Upside down," as a description of what is happening all over the country, is insufficient. Believe it or not, one migrant arrested the next day is actually at Rikers Prison on a 15-thousand-dollar bond! MLR)

On February 20, 2024, the New York Post did an expose article on the New York immigration crisis that richly deserves mention for all the wrong reasons. New York Mayor Eric Adams announced a new first of its kind 2.5-billion-dollar debit card program which is designed to assign each immigrant in the city of New York up to 10, 000 thousand dollars to use without any restrictions. No identification would be required and there would be no fraud control. Children under eighteen would get a card with parental consent. These cards would be usable at any city ATM. To justify the program, the mayor said that "migrants staying at city hotels and shelters don't eat all their food."

On average, some 5,000 meals a day are thrown away. Some of the meals are inedible for a variety of reasons but the main reason is that migrants simply do not care for the food. To make matters even more disgusting, the no bid contract was awarded to a minority contractor that has little prior experience in this type of market. Mobility Capital Finance stands to make fifty-three million dollars in fees in the twelve-month program. The contract ends on January 1, 2025. It is funded by the city.

(This is a wide-open program we will all be reading about in the next eighteen months for massive fraud, theft and sale of cards, unauthorized purchases, etc. It is not like New York is not already drowning in undocumented immigrants. The city is on the verge of collapse, but the left-wing progressives are blind to the reality. Two months into this new welfare program, you must believe that the word is out. Come to New York, live well!! MLR)

Chapter 3 - The Drug Scourge

On December 14, 2023, seven fourth graders in an Amherst, Virginia elementary schools were sickened after consuming gummy balls brought to the school by a student. Soon after all seven students got sick and experienced nausea, vomiting, headaches, and muscle spasms. All the students were taken to a local hospital and treated. Several of the students were treated with Narcan, used to treat drug overdoses. All recovered. The candy was tested at the hospital and found to be laced with the synthetic drug fentanyl. Fortunately, no one died. A police investigation resulted in the arrest of two people, a 26-year-old woman, thought to be the mother of the child who brought the candy to school and a 50-year-old adult male who was a convicted felon and in possession of a handgun when arrested. The two were arrested in a home where a large quantity of drugs were found.

(I do not know what must happen before we take definitive action to put an end to this type of incident, which occurs all too often in this country. It looks like the adults were drug sellers and the nine-year-old took what he thought was a bag of gummies to share with his friends at school. At least in this case, no bail for the felon who was on parole anyway. I cannot help but be cynical. This drug scourge is completely out of control and will get worse because the federal government, which should be a leader in presenting and

passing strict anti-drug legislation, is doing nothing. And the states are not far behind. MLR)

Across the country, many "blue" states and municipalities within those states – Portland, Oregon; Seattle, Washington; New York City, New York; San Francisco, California- have for years been pursuing a philosophy of decriminalizing drug use and possession, offering drug addicts sites to safely shoot up drugs under supervision without fear of arrest. Welfare subsidies and services for drug addicts were a key piece of the effort. The idea was that addicts represented a health issue and should not be imprisoned for possession of small amounts of drugs.

What has developed over time in most of these cities is a degradation of communities where these addicts spend time together, which is in downtown areas of these municipalities. Tent cities are the norm. As a result, taxpayers and businesses have fled these areas causing loss of business, jobs, and much needed tax revenues for these communities.

In a New York Times article on this subject, dated December 12, 2023, the city of Portland, Oregon was highlighted for the major policy changes it wants to make "Right now" to change the direction and philosophy of dealing with the addiction issue that is destroying downtown Portland and surrounding neighborhoods.

In 2020, a progressive Oregon legislature passed a wide-ranging drug decriminalization law, Measure 110, the nation's first law of its type to allow small amounts of drugs for individual use, drugs like heroin, fentanyl, and methamphetamine. Jail would not be used as punishment and new investments in drug treatment and life support like housing, would be made. Also, addicts would be able to go to a safe location to shoot up their drugs under supervision and would receive treatment if an overdose occurred. Over the last four years in Portland, the program has spun out of control. In the Portland area, five hundred drug related deaths occur annually. Area crime is up, and city residents are complaining about the declining quality of their lives in the city. People and businesses are moving out. The same problems are a new reality in San Francisco where drug users are being arrested and prosecuted; in Seattle, a new law just passed prohibits possession of drugs and use of drugs in public places; and across Oregon and Portland in particular, Governor Tina Kotek wants to ban public drug use, give local police departments more resources to control drug distribution and restore criminal penalties for drug possession, sale, and drug related crime. There is strong support for this legislation in the Oregon legislature.

(I wrote about Harm Reduction in Chapter 3. There was no question that this type of treatment modality was going to spring up in those states and municipalities where progressive liberals ruled the roost. After just a few years of it in Portland, government officials have had a big change of heart. It does not work there, and it is not working anywhere; at least that is what the media is saying, often quoting the very officials who supported the concept years ago. No community, no state, no national government could afford for long the outrageous costs that come from subsidizing drug habits and living requirements of hundreds of thousands of addicts until they die, and that is exactly about what we are discussing. What has changed the landscape is fentanyl and xylazine. These two drugs, since they arrived on the scene just a few years ago, are devastating our society and country. There is little chance of recovery from them. People on these two drugs must be taken off the street when arrested and offered long term in-patient treatment when allowed by federal and state laws, which must be upgraded "Right now" to deal with the drug scourge devastating the United States. MLR)

On January 8, 2024, law enforcement agents from Ecuador and Columbia, with help from the U. S. Drug Enforcement Agency (DEA), broke up a cartel drug pipeline that funneled five tons of cocaine a month to the United States and Europe. Two brothers of the "Los Curva" cartel in Ecuador, Hader, and Dairon Cuero, were captured along with members of the Sinaloa cartel in Mexico and several major players from the Balkan region of Europe.

(This cartel made an estimated two billion dollars a year in profit. This action was a good control measure for sure, but it will never be the cure because there is none if demand for cocaine, heroin and the like remains at staggering levels. That has been and is presently the case in the U. S. and Europe. MLR)

On Friday, January 12, 2024, the U.S. Supreme Court indicated it would rule on a case challenging the homeless camps and drug addicted residents in these camps and related crime and squalor. In 2018, the progressive, left-leaning 9th Circuit Court of Appeals ruled that depriving the homeless population of their right to live on public grounds would be "cruel and unusual treatment." The 9th Circuit Court of Appeals covers most Western states. As a result of that ruling, cities like Phoenix, AR, San Francisco and Los Angeles, CA, Portland, OR and Seattle, WA were powerless to do anything to control what has become an uncontrollable problem. The suit was filed by the city of Grants Pass, Oregon. Their suit was filed because of "out of control" drug abuse activities on the public streets of the city, drug overdoses twenty-four hours a day, violent drug related crime, open-air drug sales, public indecency, and numerous homeless encampments. Also, downtown businesses are closing, and people are moving out of the city as a result. In the city of Portland, 75% of the homeless population refused any help when asked and in San Francisco, 54% did the same.

(I blame progressive judges, liberal legislatures, and "blue" communities across the country for allowing this to go on in the first place. This movement is on the downside thankfully because many "blue" communities have had enough. People are fed up and let the ruling elites know it. Here is another example of how the individual vote can make a difference. This kind of behavior does not happen in most communities, thankfully. The fact that many impacted

communities in this country are attempting to reverse this situation is a good thing. The Supreme Court decision is due in June of 2024. If the Supreme Court rules in favor of Grants Pass, other cities impacted by the horror of open drug sales and use and the resultant negative behavior, will hopefully follow suit and go to the courts or local and state legislative bodies for relief. MLR)

On January 30, 2024, Vertex Pharmaceutical out of Boston, Massachusetts announced that it had developed an experimental drug, VX-548, which prevents pain signals from the source of pain from reaching the brain and spinal cord, thus preventing the possibility of addiction. Vertex has been working on the development of this drug for the past twenty years. Trials on the efficacy of the drug, i.e., side effects and impact, have been very successful. The pill was designed to treat moderate to severe pain, the degree of pain that relates to the aftereffects of surgery. The company is now running trials on the treatment of acute pain with this drug. Two decades ago, the widespread prescribing of COX-2 inhibitors, like oxycodone, to deal with post-surgical pain, created a massive drug addiction problem in this country. In recent months, multi-billion-dollar settlements by some of the largest pharmaceutical companies, like Pharma, exonerated public health officials who took the position that these drugs were anything but safe, as advertised by these companies with impunity for decades. Twenty years ago, everybody was making a fortune off these drugs-companies that produced them: lobbyists who protected the trade from Congressional action, and doctors who prescribed them. Vertex said it would apply to the Federal Drug Administration (FDA) by mid-year for approval to market the drug.

(In a sea of bad news related to just about everything covered in this book, this news release by Vertex has the potential to save hundreds of thousands of lives, perhaps millions over the long term, who have to face serious surgery for one reason or another, by simply avoiding the use of COX-2 inhibitors and taking the option,

the Vertex pill, VX-548 or what it eventually will be called once on the market, to recover from post- surgical pain. It is possible that the pill will reduce the use of narcotics for pain management in most people. The pill is non-addictive based on the way it works. I am praying hard that this is a major breakthrough in the fight against drug addiction. The issues of cost and availability will have to be worked out, but I believe any issues will be resolved quickly or else. MLR)

This drug, VX-548, could be the deliverance for thousands of construction workers in this country who are injured on the job, have surgery and get addicted while using prescribed opiates during recovery. Opiates are often prescribed for construction injuries because of the physical nature of the work. In 2020, there were 162 overdose deaths per 100,000 construction workers in this country. Casual substance abuse in the industry is rife and often leads to addiction. The Center for Disease Control (CDC), in a report released in August 2023, stated that overdose deaths in the construction industry were the highest of any industry in the country. It has gotten so bad that most construction sites now stock NARCAN on site and hold periodic discussion meetings with workers on site to emphasis the seriousness of the problem.

Chapter 4 - The National Debt

I was doing some research on a completely different subject when I came across this unbelievable factoid, a gift from President Biden. Late in fiscal year 2022, Biden granted the huge sum of 38.5 billion dollars to the Teamsters Union Central State Pension Fund, which was on the verge of bankruptcy. Some 350,000 union workers in the Midwest were in danger of losing their pensions or having them reduced permanently. The money was drawn from the American Rescue Plan Act (ARPA) passed in 2021. The pension fund in question has been under federal management for the past forty years, ever since the Mafia and Jimmy

Hoffa bled the fund dry back in the sixties and seventies. Despite federal oversight, this fund still managed to collapse over time anyway.

(This is an outrageous gift that the taxpayers of this country cannot afford. I could support a loan, but this was an outright gift. There are over two hundred union and private pension funds that are in serious trouble "Right now" and they got zero! The Department of Justice (DOJ) should get involved here because 38.5 billion dollars is a lot of money and could have been used for better things like immigration control, drug rehabilitation, reducing the national debt, improving our criminal justice system, job training, military readiness, climate control, or a million other things. MLR)

In early January 2024, the national debt increased to 34,136 billion dollars for the first time in this country's history. The interest that will be paid in FY 2024 will exceed one trillion dollars! The budget deficit at the end of FY 2024 is expected to exceed two trillion dollars! The Congressional Budget Office (CBO) indicated that these estimates may be low since there is still no federal budget for FY 23-24 as of March 15, 2024. This has investors worried that the 27 trillion-dollar Treasury Bond market, where this country borrows it money, may suffer from reduced demand which could result in a massive sell-off of held bonds. Foreign countries currently hold seven trillion dollars of U. S. debt. This country's three biggest obligations are Medicare, Social Security and the interest paid on our debt.

(The handwriting is on the wall. The current budget stand-off is due to exactly this issue: Biden spending is out of control, fraud in government programs, like Medicare, is out of control and the money we give away to foreign countries that hate us is out of control. This cannot continue and this is why right-wing Republicans in the House are forcing the issue by refusing to fund the war in Ukraine, the war in Israel or the potential for war in Taiwan. What the Republicans want is reduced spending and some

definitive polices which will end the immigration debacle at our borders now, "Right now" not a year from now. We are six months into the FY 2024 budget year with no budget. MLR)

(Another Continuing Resolution which funds the government until early March was passed in the Congress on Thursday, January 18, 2024. No agreement on funding Ukraine or Israel and no decisions on the border. There is a proposed budget amount under consideration, 1.66 trillion dollars which the radical right wing of the House Republican Party, the "Freedom Caucus," has declared a total failure. House Speaker Mike Johnson has said he is through with Continuing Resolutions to run the government (but not yet). This is a very dangerous situation to be in, in an election year. There are frantic negotiations ongoing to get a budget figure that can become the actual budget everyone can agree on. That plus new border policies and billions of dollars in war funding for Israel and Ukraine. I am dubious but miracles do happen. MLR)

On February 29, 2024, the Congress agreed to a stopgap spending bill to once again at the very last second, avert a partial government shutdown. The measure extended the shutdown from March 1 to March 8, 2024, for six major spending bills and six additional bills were extended from March 8 to March 22, 2024.

(This is not even a process anymore. It is a crime or should be. This is madness that exists in our political structure in Washington because of ego and hatred. The extremes of government are in control. The people be damned. Our votes in November can change all of it. We just must believe this is true and that we can make it happen. MLR)

On March 6, 2024, the House of Representatives passed a finance bill to fund six of the twelve major spending bills required to operate the government through September 2024. The 460-billion-dollar appropriation was salvaged by wide support by the Democratic minority which once again frustrated the hard right Republicans who did everything, they could do to defeat the bill and cause a partial shutdown. The Senate immediately passed the bill and President Biden signed it before the March 8 midnight deadline. The remaining six bills must be signed off by March 22, 2024, or a partial shutdown will occur. If that happens, Defense monies would be frozen.

(This process of bedlam is a poor substitute for a normal budget cycle which is often chaotic. I doubt there will be a formal budget approved this FY. What is worse is the fact that this Congress included in this bill, 12.6 billion dollars in earmarks from both sides of the aisle. Earmarks are back and they are nothing more than the pet projects of wasteful spending legislators bring back to their districts to garner votes, especially in an election year. MLR)

Chapter 5 - Corruption

On December 12, 2023, the New York Post published a good news article on corruption. The late Ponzi scheme king Bernie Madoff, who was highlighted in this book in Chapter 5, and who swindled 41,000 investors out of billions of dollars, has managed to pay another 158 million dollars to these investors through the Madoff Victim Fund. The total amount paid to investors through the fund, set up a decade ago, now totals 4.22 billion dollars. Investors have so far recouped 91% of their losses. It is anticipated that a final payment will be made by the end of 2024.

(It is nice to see a happy ending once in a while in the face of a massive fraud committed over decades. This guy embezzled sixty-five billion dollars from investors spanning 127 countries and 49 U.S. states. The level of greed on both sides of the fence in this fraud cannot be expressed in words. MLR)

In another good news article on corruption, the Springfield Republican, in its December 8, 2023, edition, printed a story about the Harvard Medical School morgue which was highlighted in Chapter 5. After it was revealed that morgue employees had been selling body parts on the street for approximately five years, Harvard University requested an investigation. The newly released 26-page report recommended a new oversight structure and an overhaul of its record-keeping and cadaver-tracking systems. The report also recommended the university establish an operational committee and governing board to increase oversight of the morgue. It also suggested the school require ethics training for morgue employees and stringent employment screening, including background checks.

(Harvard University has been in the spotlight a lot lately. You must wonder if the culture there has gone off the rails. Arrogance is one thing but the anti-Semitic scandal that has erupted on this country's university and college campuses and at Harvard, and the selling of cadaver body parts on the Harvard campus over a period of years, is something else altogether. Still, these are two good examples of how terrible criminal behavior can be managed in the long term and hopefully impact future behavior. MLR)

On February 14, 2024, the Springfield Republican published an article concerning twelve lawsuits filed by forty-seven families impacted by the Harvard Medical School's Anatomical Gift Program. Judge Kenneth Salinger dismissed all lawsuits deciding that the school and two Harvard employees had immunity under a Massachusetts law governing body donations. The Massachusetts law was patterned after the federal Uniform Anatomical Gift Act. Lawyers for the families indicated they may appeal. The judge did rule that a third employee, the program's manager, was still subject to the civil suit because his behavior was so egregious that it fell outside the Uniform Act. He also was arrested on criminal charges in the case.

(Once again, people escape responsibility. Once again institutions like Harvard escape responsibility. This horrific practice of selling body parts went on for decades and Harvard successfully claimed it knew nothing about it. It does make me angry. An appeal will be expensive and may produce an unfavorable opinion for the families. Deep down, I do believe that Harvard did, in fact, take some type of action against some key employees who should have known what was going on. MLR)

A Blockbuster article, put out by the New York Times on January 6, 2024, told of the pending civil trial against the National Rifle Association (NRA) and its decades old CEO Wayne LaPierre. The case had been brought by Letitia James, the attorney general of the state of New York, the same person going after Donald Trump. The state is alleging that LaPierre and three other top executives of the powerful gun rights group, used the NRA as their personal piggy bank to fund luxury vacations, rent private jets and buy expensive dinners, jewelry purchases, clothing at the finest boutiques, world travel, all to the tune of 64 million dollars over three years!! As a result of this massive fraud, the NRA is facing bankruptcy. Revenue was down 44% last year; membership has gone down to 4.2 million from a high of six million; legal costs are at the 10-million-dollar level and going up.

LaPierre resigned effective January 31, 2024.

(I was absolutely stunned when I saw this article. I had no idea that the NRA was facing destruction. This was the main organization that has prevented any meaningful gun legislation to pass in the U.S. Congress for years because the NRA lobbyists had paid off most of the key senators and representatives who could have passed meaningful and effective legislation going back thirty years, the amount of time LaPierre was the CEO. And why a civil case? When will the feds arrest him and his friends on criminal charges? Why is it that too many of these people never get arrested? MLR)

On February 24, 2024, LaPierre and two of his partners in crime were found guilty of financial misconduct and corruption. LaPierre was ordered to pay the NRA 5.4 million dollars. He had already paid 1.1 million dollars but still owes 4.35 million dollars. The case was first presented in court in 2020. At the time of his departure from the NRA, he was earning 2.2 million dollars annually.

(The final disposition in this case is not even remotely a control mechanism. It is a joke. LaPierre and his friends should have been criminally charged and sent to prison for a long time upon conviction. LaPierre is through and that is certainly a good thing and his wife will not be getting any more 10-thousand-dollar pedicures, and he is through spending over 225 thousand dollars for fancy suits at a Hollywood boutique the last couple of years. But do not count on it. However, he is certainly through handing out millions upon millions of dollars to members of Congress over his thirty years in power. This is a good thing. Who got all the money? How about Sen. Mitt Romney (R-UT). He got 13 million + dollars from the NRA over the years; Sen. Thom Tillis (R-NC) got 4 million + dollars; Sen. Marco Rubio(R-FL) got 3 million + dollars; Sen. Mitch McConnell (R-KY) got 1 million + dollars; Sen. Richard Burr (R-NC) got 6 million + dollars and Sen. Roy Blount (R-MO) got 4.5 million dollars, to name just a few. MLR)

Pandemic related fraud is continuing at a torrid pace if you believe an editorial published in the Springfield Republican of February 4, 2024. In 2023, the Associated Press did an analysis on the COVID spending spree, which I covered in this book. The bottom line was estimated theft totaling 280 billion dollars looted from the various federal programs during the pandemic. Another 123 billion dollars was simply misspent. Many experts considered these figures on the low side. The paper went on to provide some recent sobering data that indicates the fraud continues today in one major program, the Employee Retention Credit Act, which provides tax breaks to employers who continued to pay their employees during the pandemic. The projected cost of this program was fifty-five billion dollars. Today the cost is 220 billion dollars. The IRS has over one million claims pending and most are considered fraudulent. The IRS also has active investigations into untold billions of dollars stolen. What is astounding is the fact that employers can submit their applications through tax year 2025.

(I am at a loss for words. It is simply incomprehensible that the Congress can sit there and do nothing. At the rate of theft from just these pandemic programs, I would not be surprised if the federal courts of the land will be disposing of these cases for the next decade, just as they will deal with all the January 6th cases. The convicted offenders deserve jail time, and the American taxpayers want and deserve restitution and hefty fines that must be paid before any of these crooks are released from prison. MLR)

On Tuesday, February 7, 2024, you could have your pick of major corruption stories breaking out across the country. I chose two that broke in New York City, both representative of how persistent these types of crime are today everywhere it seems. The New York City Housing Authority (NYCHA) is the biggest housing authority in the country, overseeing 335 developments in its five boroughs. These developments house hundreds of thousands of people, mostly low-income people who qualify for rental assistance. The case involved seventy housing supervisors, superintendents, assistant superintendents, and other management level employees throughout the boroughs who were tasked with managing a massive operation that ensured the safety of residents and the maintenance of numerous housing units in the city. They earned an average of one hundred thousand dollars annually plus overtime and great benefits. These seventy employees were indicted by a federal grand jury on numerous counts of bribery and extortion in a pay-to-play enterprise that started ten years ago and involved over two million dollars in bribes paid out by willing contractors.

The operation keyed in on no-bid contracts for emergency repairs required to keep the housing units livable. These contracts were managed by the housing supervisors and superintendents, who turned it into a multi-million-dollar gravy train. Over thirteen million dollars in contracts were awarded in a decade but some experts believe that was only the tip of the iceberg. Contractors who would not participate got no work. For years contractors and residents complained but nobody listened until a few years ago when the feds got involved.

(Contractors paid 10-20% of the contract cost to get the contract. Things came to a head when some supervisors started demanding more money. This is called greed committed by the very people paid good money to make sure stuff like this did not happen. Some of the offenders will take a plea deal and some will go to trial, and some will see the inside of a prison, but I will bet good money that prison sentences will be short, and restitution will be made. Imagine what will happen if all seventy crooks want a trial. The critical concern is the major reorganization of the NYCHA, which many public and private organizations have been demanding for years. Change is needed to manage the problem. MLR)

In yet another case, the New York development firm, HFZ Capital Corporation, presided over by Nir Meir, and four associates, was indicted by Manhattan District Attorney Alvin L. Bragg on state embezzlement charges involving the theft of millions of dollars from investors who believed the company was a legitimate enterprise. In 2019, HFZ managed over ten billion dollars in property in New York and other areas. A construction company, Omnibuild, was also involved in the conspiracy which covered a span of 5-8 years before the operation crashed when the pandemic required many people to work at home and leave the big office buildings in the big cities empty. Bragg's office indicated the investigation is ongoing and "many more arrests are anticipated."

(This is big time fraud, a crime that will exist until the end of time, but it can be managed if justice does prevail after the court maneuvering is done and guilt is determined. This case will take years after all the appeals. People who get involved in this type of serious economic crime must receive long prison sentences. It is the only way to manage this problem. Enough said. MLR)

In early January of 2024, the New York Times did a piece on Linda Hennis of Chicago, a retired nurse, who was reviewing her monthly Medicare statement when she noticed a company she never heard of had been paid twelve thousand dollars for sending her two thousand urinary catheters. She never received the catheters and does not use them. She filed a complaint to discover that Medicare was in the throes of trying to stop a multi-billion-dollar catheter fraud. The company was called "Pretty in Pink Boutique (PIPB)" and was in Texas. In 2023, over 450,000 persons receiving Medicare were billed for catheters; in 2022, 50,000 were billed for catheters. In addition, Medicare investigators discovered that seven high volume companies involved in the catheter business were involved. An organization, the National Association of Accountable Care Organizations, alerted Medicare to the problem.

Between October 22 and December 23, PIPB billed Medicare 267 million dollars for catheters and Medicare paid it! PIPB is registered with Medicare to a street address in El Paso, Texas. The company phone goes to an auto body shop, "West Texas Body and Paint" in West Texas. An employee there said he gets dozens of phones calls every day from Medicare enrollees concerned about fraudulent billings.

The director of Medicare's Center for Program Integrity, Dara Corrigan, would not discuss the catheter situation. She did indicate that "the Medicare billing scam is one of those problems that is ever-present and ever- frustrating." She did admit that of the seven major companies involved in this catheter situation, only one had a working phone.

(I remember recently reading an article on Medicare fraud where the author claimed that Medicare did not know how much money is stolen every year. The estimate of between eight hundred billion and one trillion dollars over the last decade seemed about right. It is easy to steal from Medicare. The budget shortfall in the Medicare allocation fell short by over five billion dollars in 2023. It is exactly this kind of reality which will force this country into bankruptcy and when that happens, nobody will get paid. Take this seriously. Fraud in all types of federal programs is out of control. I do not believe a political will exists in this country to address the problem currently. MLR)

This will be the last corruption case I will present. I think I have made my point at least concerning this chapter. This last one though is a beaut! On February 13, 2024, three former executives of First Energy in Ohio and a former state public utility commissioner, were indicted on theft, bribery, and fraud charges involving a payment of 4.3 million dollars to allow First Energy to overcharge its customers. The state of Ohio is alleging that the company's chief executive and a vice-president of External Affairs, paid Mike Dowling, the chairman of the commission a bribe of 4.3 million dollars over time. The case is being called the biggest public corruption scandal in Ohio's history. The utility serves six million people. One former state legislator is already in prison in connection with this ongoing case. The scandal erupted in 2020 when the Speaker of the Ohio House of Representatives, Larry Householder, was arrested for accepting a 60-million-dollar bribe. He was convicted in 2023 and received a sentence of twenty years. In return for the bribe, Householder passed House Bill (HB) six, which provided a 1.3-billion-dollar bailout of two nuclear power plants managed by First Energy.

(This type of criminal behavior is happening all over this country non-stop. Twenty-year sentences should be the absolute minimum for this type of crime. And banishment forever from this

type of business or any business for that matter. Long prison sentences, hefty fines and complete restitution will never solve the problem but do represent very good management tools. MLR)

Chapter 6 - Climate Change

On December 7, 2023, the U. S. Energy Administration reported that exports of U. S. crude are averaging six million barrels a day. Overall domestic production has surged to a record thirteen million barrels a day.

(This is good news for a lot of people in the industry and for Americans in general. It is not good news for those who are worried that the world will come to an end in about ten years if government is not able to reduce its carbon emissions. The way it looks "Right now," the U.S. is breaking all production records in crude oil at exactly the wrong time. MLR)

It was reported in the New York Times on Tuesday, December 6, 2023, that severe and prolonged drought has forced the Panama Canal to reduce its boat traffic as low water levels from the supporting lakes have forced shipping companies to pay millions of dollars to jump the line or sail around the tips of Africa and South America at a time of high inflation and costly fuel. The other option is to just wait your turn to travel through the 50-mile waterway. The wait can take days because of a lack of water. The average number of ships traveling through the canal today is twenty-four, down from the usual thirty-eight. Rainfall in Panama was 30% below normal in 2023. The annual dry season in Panama starts in December and ends in May. The situation there will get much worse before it gets better if it ever does.

The annual COP 28 Climate Conference was held in Dubai, United Arab Emirates, from December 1-15, 2023. The interesting thing about this conference was that it was held in a country that has so much oil, it will be one hundred years before Dubai ceases oil exploration and production. In fact, the climate summit president, Al Jaber, who runs a huge state-owned oil company in Dubai, took the position that oil exploration and production are good things. This of course pissed about all the 70,000 attendees from 198 nations. Donald Trump would not have attended. Biden sent his climate guy John Kerry who, on behalf of Biden, pledged to deliver 11.4 billion dollars annually in climate assistance by 2024, if Congress agrees. Biden also attempted earlier this year to put one billion dollars into a general climate fund controlled by the United Nations, but the U.S. House blocked the attempt.

(Biden is dreaming. The amount of money he wants to give away in support of climate change is completely unrealistic currently. Further, many countries do not consider the U. S. to be reliable in its funding promises because it routinely falls far short of these promises year after year. What a mess!! MLR)

Lisa Friedman, of the New York Times, in an article dated December 16, 2023, wrote that the global agreement made in Dubai was the first time in decades that there was an agreement in principle that the culprit was the burning of coal, oil and gas. In a moment of significant compromise, governments called for "Transitioning away from fossil fuels this decade in a just, orderly, and equitable manner." Mr. Kerry, who recently resigned his position as a climate Czar in the Biden administration to work on the Biden re-election team, called the agreement the "most important decision since the Paris agreement in 2015." Many present did not agree, especially representatives of the oil rich countries in that region. Many island nations took the position that the conference did not go far enough in its commitment to transition from fossil fuels. The reality for these nations is how to continue to fight rising sea levels successfully "Right now." Former vice-president Al Gore, considered by many a serious champion of climate change, called the conference "a complete failure."

Michael L. Roeder

(Kerry made it very clear in his comments during the conference that there is a good chance for success if the countries do what they promised to do in the next decade. If it is business as usual, there will be little if any progress if promises are not kept and the money does not get committed to the levels promised. I wonder what will happen next. More promises? MLR)

In a New York Times article dated December 5, 2023, there was an article by Liz Alderman on white hydrogen, a clean, non-carbon burning fuel that releases water into the atmosphere. There is no carbon release whatsoever. A huge hydrogen reservoir had recently been discovered in eastern France. This discovery had awakened all of Europe to the possibilities of commercial production on a large scale, as well as the possibility of additional reservoirs on the continent. The fact is that, on an annual basis, seventy million metric tons of hydrogen are produced commercially worldwide. Producing commercial hydrogen involves energy splitting water into hydrogen and oxygen, a process that results in gray oxygen. In Colorado, Koloma, an energy company, is actively probing for hydrogen in the Midwest. In the long term, the key is cost and the marketability of the finished product. Green hydrogen, produced by wind and solar, is highly subsidized in the U. S. Hydrogen power, or gray hydrogen, is not.

(Experts predict that gray hydrogen could substitute for 50% of carbon emissions worldwide. Let us assume for just one second that is possible, even if it is 25 years down the road. This could be the energy source which saves the planet. I am hopeful we do not pass up an opportunity here. Tremendous amounts of money have been spent over the last decade, trillions on solar, wind, and other renewables, but I have not read much about hydrogen. MLR)

Energy history was made the last week of November in New York State when the first completed turbine of 12 turbines that will make up South Fork Wind in Long

Island Sound, the first large-scale offshore wind farm to go online in the United States. When the project is completed, it will produce 132 megawatts of electricity, enough to power 70,000 homes. The energy is transmitted through an undersea cable to a substation in East Hampton, NY, then distributed to customers of the Long Island Power Authority.

(This is good news for energy advocates, especially when it concerns wind turbine projects which are being cancelled all over the globe "Right now" because of high borrowing costs, shortage of building materials, and the increasing costs of production. Wind power must work in the long term. It will survive if it becomes profitable enough for investors. Let us pray for a good outcome. MLR)

The New York Times Magazine, published every Sunday, released an in-depth article on the continent of Africa, emphasizing its place in the climate change crusade currently underway in the world. It was the most sobering and depressing piece I have read to date on our climate, vis-à-vis Africa's role to play in the climate solution.

First, the fifty-four countries that make up the African Continent have huge infrastructure and cultural problems and many of the countries are corrupt beyond imagination. Several African countries were highlighted in Chapter 5 on corruption in the world but it was only the tip of the iceberg.

Six hundred million Africans lack electrical power. Sanitation is primitive, even in many of the major cities. A never-ending baby boom limits progress in many countries. There is a youth boom in Africa "Right now." The median age is nineteen, which means half of the population is under nineteen and half the population is over nineteen. Unemployment among the young is rampant. As a result of a lack of jobs and the insistence of old, corrupt leaders to steal, migration out of Africa, is at an all-time high. The U.S. is seeing this phenomenon firsthand "Right now." Many countries are experiencing military coups which, in effect, replace one corrupt regime with another. Democracy as a form of government and a way of life, is at its lowest point. Africa is still primarily a developing agricultural continent, with little manufacturing capability. The continent is being ravaged by every climate extreme you can name.

Despite all the negatives, many African countries are working hard to improve their environments. African organizations like the Organization of African Unity (OAU) have established two major priorities for their members - jobs for young Africans and climate improvements. They are looking for money to accomplish both. China is deeply involved with grants and loans to several countries looking to establish manufacturing businesses and climate change systems. In Kenya, engineers have developed a machine that can extract carbon from the air. While this is still in the development stage, if it works, could be a world saving climate tool. In Namibia, a ten-billion-dollar green hydrogen producing plant is under construction. A multi-billion-dollar solar tower was recently constructed in Morocco.

Africa just happens to have 78% of the world's current cobalt supply, which is needed to produce electric vehicles. There is a commitment to take advantage of this reality by bringing electric car production capability to the continent. Jobs would be created, and many Africans put to work. This is critical because in 2022 African migrants living abroad, sent home ninety-six billion dollars in currency. One area of remarkable growth in the last decade in Africa has been the film and music industries.

(The situation on the African continent has good and bad news. Quite frankly, the bad news far exceeds any good news that you read about. Africa is this huge continent that is experiencing war, civil unrest, horrific climate disasters, disease and death, massive corruption, and an exploding population all at the same time. Climate management in Africa will be slowed by all the above and a

dearth of funding so necessary for just that part of the problem to become manageable. It seems to me that there are a number of far more serious issues that must be solved first. MLR)

In a New York Times article published on February 14, 2024, major U. S. gas exporters to Asia are planning to send that natural gas so plentiful in the United States, to Asia by using a pipeline being constructed now along the U, S. –Mexican border. One such facility in Mexico is complete and should be ready to accept gas products by the end of 2025. The terminal is called Energia Costa Azul along Mexico's west coast. It is undergoing a 2-billion-dollar upgrade at the present time. The project has already been approved by the Biden administration, which once again has pissed off climate control activists. This new delivery capability will allow exporters to avoid using the Panama Canal altogether since terminals on Mexico's west coast will be able to load ships and deliver directly to Asia. This will save huge amounts of transportation costs and time as well. In all, five terminals are planned for Mexico's west coast. Export volume could realistically double in the next four years.

(One step forward, two steps back. This project will be an economic boom for the United States. Asia is looking to this country for natural gas to gradually replace its reliance on coal. China is the leader. Biden is hot for the issue one day and against it the next. He has recently put a pause on new unapproved LNG projects until the impact of these projects on the climate can be assessed. This makes the activists happy; at the same time, it makes Asian countries nervous. It is vintage Biden behavior. A final note: the natural gas that is projected to ship from the Azul terminal has already been contracted out (sold) for the next ten years. Good news for the U.S. economy and Treasury, bad news for the climate. MLR)

Who knew? This country is about to embark on a new national energy strategy that centers on the development of nuclear energy, which does not emit greenhouse gases. On February 28, 2024, the U. S. House of Representatives passed the Atomic Energy Advancement Act by a vote of 365 to 36. In Washington, there is now broad support for the development of nuclear power in this country.

(It is a well-accepted reality that many of the existing nuclear power plants in this country are old and need upgrading. I hope the legislation provides funding support for this. The cost of this legislation would seem to be staggering in its scope and when compared to all the other costs already identified in this book, I am again wondering where all this money is going to come from and how existing funds will be expended? MLR)

Another Biden flip-flops? On February 29, 2024, the Environmental Protection Agency (EPA) exempted operating gas plants in this country from a requirement to capture their carbon dioxide emissions by 2040. Major industries and several powerful Democrats in the U.S. Congress raised hell over this climate control issue. The environment advocates went crazy again because this means the carbon emissions from these plants will continue to pollute the environment for many, many years to come. 2040-forget it. How about 2140?

The Smoke House Creek fire in the Texas Panhandle, which started on February 21, 2024, has burned over one million acres, killed two people and 4,000 cattle, destroyed five hundred structures and is only 15 % contained. It is the largest fire ever recorded in the state of Texas. The damage will be catastrophic. Fires have also been reported in Nebraska and Kansas. All the fires are strengthened by ferocious winds. In the Sierra Nevada Mountains in California and Nevada, up to twelve feet of snow has fallen since March 1, 2024. Yosemite National Park has been closed, highways shut down with hundreds of trucks and cars stranded in place, most ski resorts shut down and people unable to dig out of their own homes. Another monster storm is expected to drop at least five feet of snow in the region.

(If you believe the experts, this weather is the new norm. And how about the new lake that now exists in Death Valley because of all the monster rainstorms that have hit the California coast in the last month? That has never happened before but will now often. This new norm will kill thousands, injure thousands, kill cattle and wildlife, destroy property and structures and property of all types. We are in big trouble here. I am not sure we are doing enough; I am not sure it would make any difference. MLR)

Chapter 7 - War

On December 13, 2023, Congress passed the 3,100-page 2024 Defense Authorization Bill calling for the expenditure of 886 billion dollars this fiscal year.

As expected, it contained no military funding for Ukraine or Israel. Biden wanted 105 billion dollars for these two countries. House Republicans refused to put the aid for Israel and Ukraine in the bill because Biden refused to get serious about immediate immigration reform. Senate Republicans want a separate bill for 105 billion dollars to be immediately considered but House Speaker Mike Johnson indicated that a decision on that funding proposal would not happen anytime soon in the House.

(This situation could be a disaster for this country and the world. The Republicans have tied together two very serious problems for Americans in particular, war funding and border funding. On the one hand, the majority of people in this country believe the immigration situation is completely out of control. Biden has lost control of it and has decided to let in the whole world at a cost factor that is not sustainable. Republicans want to gain control of the problem and they will overnight if Trump is elected in 2024. Trump has said recently and repeatedly that he will solve the undocumented immigration problem immediately after being sworn in. I believe he will. However, that is a year away. The war in Ukraine is at a point where our failure to continue providing military and financial aid could prove fatal to that country's war effort. Indeed, just today, December 15, 2023, the European Union announced that a 52-billion-dollar military aid package for Ukraine was voted down by Hungary. So, in just a few days it looks like 113 billion dollars of military aid to Ukraine is instead heading for thin air. Fortunately, on February 2, 2024, Hungary gave in and voted with most European Union members to pass the package. This takes a lot of pressure off Ukraine until the Spring. Still, if other countries start to fade away, Russia will win the war and eventually move on to other countries Putin is interested in. This would surely cause a war on the continent of Europe and who knows where else. If our military aid to Israel is interrupted, the battle there will continue but may be toned down for temporary lack of war funds here and there. This will prolong the war in Gaza and change Israel's plans for Hezbollah in Lebanon and the Palestinian Authority in the West Bank. If this does happen, that means continued assaults on Israel by these terrorist groups whenever they choose. Hamas and Hezbollah must be destroyed if Israel expects peace for decades down the road. The Palestinian Authority will need to be reoriented on its role in that part of the world and Israel is the right country to do just that, but they will need our help to do it right and thoroughly. MLR)

 U. S. Senate and White House negotiators are meeting "Right now" before Christmas break to come to some agreement on border policy changes which House Republican would find acceptable, for a military aid bill for Israel and Ukraine to go forward in the Congress. It is evident now that Biden is getting hammered on all sides by his lack of attention to what has become a national disgrace-the southern border immigration onslaught. To begin with, Latino lawmakers have been left outside the core negotiating group and the "Dream Act" is off the table for discussion. Already, immigration advocates are criticizing the process, claiming the proposals would undermine U.S. long term commitment to accepting immigrants escaping persecution. One proposal under consideration would allow border officials to easily send migrants back to Mexico without letting them seek asylum. Detention of migrants attempting to enter the country illegally, is also under consideration.

(Does this sound familiar? Trump sent millions back to Mexico and he will do it again. What about the millions of undocumented immigrants already in this country? What about the tens of thousands at the border "Right now"? Are we just going to let them all in as well? What about the three million immigrants who have asylum cases pending in our courts "Right now"? And if we do come to some agreement, what the American people get out of it is the opportunity to send Ukraine and Israel 105 billion dollars in monetary aid we will have to borrow. As a country, we are so fucked. MLR)

On Tuesday, February 13, 2024, the U. S. Senate passed a foreign aid bill to support Israel, Ukraine, and Taiwan after many months of negotiations. The measure now goes to the House for a vote.

(What a waste of time, money, and effort. The Republican controlled House will vote it down primarily because the measure does not have any provisions for border control. Nothing. But the Senate Republicans will claim a victory because they stood up and voted the measure of support for our allies, anyway, knowing it would fail in the House. Please remember, it is the fifth month of FY 2024 and we still do not have a federal budget. Complete bullshit. MLR)

Another corruption scandal occurred in Ukraine on December 24, 2023, when the Ukrainian government announced that it has arrested a senior Defense ministry official in a 40-million-dollar embezzlement on a fraudulent purchase of artillery shells. The contract was valued at 140 million dollars and was supposed to produce artillery shells for the Ukrainian army. These very shells are currently in short supply and represent the primary weapon system now used during the winter months by both sides. The arrest was made by the country's anti-corruption unit which was formed by President Zelensky when he came into office. To date, no shells have been delivered. Somehow, this unnamed ministry official managed to divert forty million dollars into his personal account initially without detection. This is a serious blow to the country's war effort since Zelensky's recent multi-billion-dollar request for additional military assistance from the United States is currently tied up in Congress.

(Donald Trump has said many times recently that he is opposed to further funding of the Ukrainian war effort. If he is elected, I believe he will end or reduce funding. This would lead to other countries following suit. Some countries have already ended or reduced their funding levels. Ukraine cannot succeed without this aid. I have said several times in this book that Ukraine will defeat itself if it cannot end this vicious cycle of corruption by high-ranking officials in Zelensky's administration. It never ends. This is not a management issue. This is not about limiting the amount of money that could be stolen in a fiscal year and somehow be acceptable or tolerated. This corruption must end. People who get arrested for stealing millions should be tried as war criminals and shot if found guilty. That would have some impact, hopefully. MLR)

On February 29, 2024, Serhiy Pashinsky, a major player in the procurement of weapons for the Ukrainian war effort, was arrested in a 25-million-dollar fuel buying scheme through a company he owned six years ago in 2018. He was a former member of the Ukrainian Parliament and was under suspicion for years. In 2019, President Zelensky publicly called him a crook. Yet, when the war broke out, he was called back into government and given major responsibilities in weapons procurement. He posted a 7-million-dollar bond. Charges are pending.

Today, our allies hold over three hundred billion dollars in frozen Russian assets which Russia cannot touch. This money, at one time when everyone was on friendlier terms, represented Russia's international reserves. The United States, not surprisingly, wants to give that money to Ukraine to fight the Russians. How ironic if this ever happens. Many allies want to do the same thing, and some even want to go after funds deposited outside of Russia by corrupt oligarchs who support Putin in his current war effort. Germany recently seized 790 million dollars from a Frankfurt bank in bed with a Russian financial firm. There is currently much research being done by the United States, Switzerland, Belgium, France, and Germany to determine what is permissible under international law. In the U. S. the feeling is that Congressional action would be necessary. Right now, it would be impossible to believe that the Democrats and Republicans could pull it off.

(I think it will happen, but it may take way too much time to help the Ukrainian war effort soon. It is needed "Right now." MLR)

In Taiwan on January 14, 2024, Lai Ching-te was elected the next president of that country, capturing 40% of the vote. His party, the Democratic Progressive Party (DPP), is a staunch advocate for independence from China. China, prior to the election, had warned the people of Taiwan that "the election was a war or peace choice" to make. China's leader, XI Jinping, has promised the Chinese people that unification of Taiwan is his highest priority during his tenure.

(This election victory could come at a very high price for Mr. Lai, who will lead Taiwan for the next four years. First, Xi Jinping does not bluff. Second, China has most definitely laid out the plan of attack on Taiwan, which in my view could come at any time. The Chinese armed forces are practicing all the time, often just off the coast of the country they will someday invade. Third, China understands what an invasion would mean-economic upheaval in China and the world, the prospect of a regional war for sure and

perhaps a world war depending on whose side the participants take. Many of the possible participants have tactical and strategic nuclear capability. Is it possible that a political agreement will be worked out in the end, after exhausting negotiations involving world powers? I doubt it. MLR)

On February 23, 2024, U.S. legislators visited Taiwan to meet with its new president elect, Lai Ching-te, who takes office in May 2024. The United States has no formal diplomatic ties with Taiwan. It does have strong military relations and gives this country a lot of foreign and military aid. U.S. Representative Mike Gallagher (R-WIS), a moderate, is not running for re-election. He has had enough. Currently, billions of dollars paid for military orders to Taiwan are backlogged and additional billions in military aid are tied up in Congress. Lai made a plea for the delivery of the military equipment and the military aid that Congress is sitting on.

(This is a sad situation. The United States is fast losing its influence in the world because of our current internal ideological differences and our enemies realize this. We cannot deliver goods to Taiwan because Ukraine was first on our list and Israel second. Taiwan comes in a distant third. I do not see most Americans concerned about this situation. I think most do not want to know. If China invades Taiwan, we will be expected to help Taiwan out with troops on the ground (we already have thousands of troops stationed in that country right now) and ships in the water and planes in the sky. Can you imagine our involvement in a three-front war? MLR)

In the early days of January 2024, American and British air forces attacked Houthi missile launch positions in Yemen after Iran backed Houthi forces ignored repeated warnings from the United State and Britain to stop attacking ships in the Red Sea headed to and from the Suez Canal. This action represents a major escalation of the conflict in Gaza. The air attacks have become a daily event.

(Sooner or later, Iran will have to be dealt with. They finance the Houthis in Yemen, Hamas in Gaza and Hezbollah in the West Bank and Lebanon. They have a presence in Syria and Iraq. The key to peace in the Middle East is the subjugation of Iran. How this happens scares me to death. All-out war in that region is a strong possibility. When Iran's demonic followers chant "from the river to the sea," they are not just chanting. They are dead serious for life. MLR)

The attack on Tower 22 in Northeast Jordan on the border with Iraq and Syria, on January 28, 2024, left three American soldiers dead and over forty-seven wounded, several seriously wounded, including a number of soldiers with traumatic brain injuries. The soldiers were members of an Army National Guard unit located in Georgia that had been mobilized and sent to Tower 22 as part of Operation Inherent Resolve. The attack was sponsored by Iran. There is an uproar from all sides except the left-wing Progressives in Congress, to take serious and definitive action against Iran immediately, knowing all too well that a full-scale retaliation from the United States could provoke a much wider conflict.

(Prior to this attack, there had been 165 attacks on American forces in that region where we have over 3,500 troops positioned. Prior to this attack, we had conducted seven retaliatory attacks on enemy positions, mostly in reaction to Houthi missile strikes on oil tankers in the Red Sea. In my day I played a lot of baseball. If I had gone 7 of 165 at bats, I would have been advised to take up another sport. What did we expect was going to happen? At some point loss of American lives was going to happen and we have an administration that is now pondering its reaction to this act of war. Iran is at war with the United States, but Biden cannot accept this proposition because Progressives do not believe in war. Iran wants a wider conflict because it is a suicidal, fanatical country that has an ingrained hatred of Jews first and the United States a close second. I wonder what Donald Trump would do in this situation. We may be less than a year away from finding out. MLR)

On February 1, 2024, the United States Air Force, which included B-1 bombers from the United States, attacked eighty-five targets in Syria and Iraq, in retaliation for the attack on Tower 22. Iran was not targeted. News agencies in those two countries did report casualties. Damage assessment by U.S. Intelligence units in the area should take a limited amount of time.

(This was clearly a required action although the delay factor gave the enemy a lot of time to clear the areas, they knew were going to get hit. The property damage will be high but enemy personnel losses will be low. The key question is: "Is this the beginning or not?" The action the militants took was a clear escalation and our reaction only feeds the fire, but it was necessary and should continue. Our Secretary of Defense was right when he said on February 2nd that "we are at a very dangerous moment in time." I could not agree more. MLR)

On February 28, 2024, the New York Times published an article on the current influence of Iran in the Iraq and Syria operational area. Since the U.S. strikes on February 2, 2024, there have been no new attacks on U.S. military forces there, indicating that Iran got the message and has persuaded the militias to cease attacks. Still, the Houthis continue to attack shipping in the Red Sea and in fact sunk a cargo ship loaded with fertilizer on February 29, 2024. Severe contamination is feared. Hezbollah continues to attach northern Israel with mostly missiles, but those attacks have been reduced in recent weeks. At the same time Israel has been attacking targets in Iran-2 main gas pipelines have been destroyed.

We learned on January 29, 2024, that twelve employees of the United Nations Relief and Works Agency (UNRWA), participated in the

October 7 massacre of 1,200 Jews in Israel. The United States and four other UN member countries immediately cut their funding of UNRWA. More member nations are expected to cut funding as well. Twelve employees have been fired. Biden has been a strong supporter of UNRWA. He resumed UNRWA funding that Trump had cut off when he was elected President of the United States. Since Biden has taken over, the U.S. has given three hundred million dollars annually to UNRWA to support Palestinian activities in Gaza. In terms of the educational climate in Gaza, it is well known that Palestinian children are taught it is okay to kill Jews and Palestinian teaching materials do not show Israel as an actual country on Middle Eastern maps.

As of March 5, 2024, southern Gaza is on the verge of a complete breakdown. Famine is real and children are dying of starvation. IDF bombings are taking a huge toll on lives and property and over 30,000 Palestinians have been killed and thousands more wounded. The situation in northern Gaza is not much better but most of the fighting is concentrated in the south. The question is when will the IDF go into Rafah where 1.5 million Palestinians are marginally existing. Hostage negations are in play, but no real progress has been made even though some experts are predicting a possible six-week truce.

(If Israel does not finish off Hamas and Hezbollah, the next massacre will certainly happen. MLR)

Chapter 8 - The Economy

A New York Post article on December 22, 2023, described a commercial real estate market in this country that is facing a default on loan payments totaling 160 billion dollars. By the end of 2025, approximately 23 months from now, 1.5 trillion dollars owned by lenders will have to be re-negotiated. A persistently high vacancy rate caused by the pandemic and high interest rates are the two main reasons for the concern. Many commercial buildings remain vacant and are falling into disrepair. This is a nationwide problem no one really anticipated. However, employees are reluctant to return to the office for a variety of reasons. Many feel the big cities are no longer safe, crime is rampant in many urban areas, and the costs of travel to and from work have increased significantly.

(A default on commercial mortgages to the tune of 160 billion dollars could cause a financial crisis comparable to the banking disaster in 2008-09. It would not be as big, but it would require government bailouts which may not be possible for a country that has a current debt of 34+ trillion dollars and increasing daily. MLR)

During the month of January 2024, the Biden Administration suffered another major setback when the Taiwan Semi-Conductor Manufacturing Company in Taiwan, announced that it was postponing production of highly sensitive computer chips at its new facility in Arizona until 2025. At the same time, Samsung, another tech giant, announced that it was postponing production at its new facility in Texas. Both companies claimed a lack of skilled labor and higher than anticipated expenses were the main reasons for the action. In August 2022, President Biden signed the CHIPS Act which provided one hundred billion dollars to manufacturers in this country to engage in the production of chips to compete with China, a country which controls the computer chip market at the present time. Under this legislation, only thirty-five million dollars has been distributed to date and it was to the BAE Systems Corporation in New Hampshire, which makes chips for the USAF's F-15 and F-35 jets.

(Biden understands the current problems with China may impact its ability to purchase these types of chips from that country if relations go completely in the toilet. Congress understood that as well, so the legislation passed quickly, which is unusual today in the U. S. Congress. However, after 17 months, the fact that only thirty-five million dollars has been distributed is not a good thing. MLR)

(It is two steps forward and one step back it seems with our economy. Inflation is cooling and the Fed recently decided not to increase interest rates, at least in the short term. But the cost of food is very high and buying a home for the average guy is just not possible with the high interest rates. Renting a place is through the roof across the country. Credit card debt and defaults are an emerging problem. It is never a good thing when people are using their credit cards to pay for housing, fuel, and food. On the other hand, unemployment is 3.7% and 9 million jobs in this country are unfilled. The government is spending way too much money and borrowing way too much money for our own good. Budget cuts are coming one way or the other, at all levels of government. Stay tuned. The radical Right in Congress is demanding big spending cuts, and the Progressive Left is too busy spending money we do not have to listen. In liberal, progressive Massachusetts, big mid-year budget spending cuts were recently announced (January 2024) and people are not happy. MLR)

Once again at the end of February 2024, Biden announced a 1.2-billion-dollar student debt forgiveness. This has brought the total forgiveness amount to 138 billion dollars for 3.9 million borrowers. Over 150,000 borrowers in the SAVE Plan had their debt wiped out if they had initially borrowed twelve thousand dollars and had been paying for at least a decade.

While many have benefited, initially Biden wanted to forgive four hundred billion dollars in student loans impacting forty-three million students, but the Supreme Court stopped that. Republicans decried the action and called it nothing more than a ploy to get votes this November. Biden made big promises at the outset but did not get the numbers he wanted, and many borrowers were angry when they realized they would not benefit. When student loan payments resumed after the pandemic, many stopped paying. This situation has turned on Biden and could hurt him in November. One prominent educator noted that "cancellation is simply transferring student debt to the taxpayer." Another big issue is the rollout of the new Free App for Federal Student Aid (FAFSA), which did not go well. Colleges have been unable to process the forms and students are not getting their loan requests approved on time for the 2024-2025 academic school year. About everyone is blaming Biden.

(The one thing the Biden Administration has proven time and time again in the last three years is that they cannot manage their way out of a paper bag opened at both ends. FAFSA is just another example. The idea that the government would pay off billions of dollars of student loans in this economy with the government 34 + trillion dollars in debt and having to borrow 6 billion dollars a day to pay bills, has always been beyond my ability to process. MLR)

Who would have thought childcare would have such a negative impact on our economy? On February 25, 2024, the National Association for the Education of Young Children released a study that described a number of trends that have increased in severity since the end of the pandemic. Among other things the following were highlighted as serious issues facing this country in this industry:

- Of 3,815 childcare business owners surveyed, one-half are enrolling fewer children due to staff shortages than before the pandemic. Workers in this industry are the lowest paid in the country.

- Owners cannot charge more because parents cannot pay more. Many parents spend one-quarter of their income on childcare.

- Working at home has changed the industry. Demand for nannies has decreased dramatically since the pandemic.

- The situation has worsened since the government stopped funding daycare operations in September 2023. From April 1, 2021 until September 2023, the government spent twenty-four billion dollars keeping daycare afloat.

- The Biden Administration has proposed sixteen billion dollars in daycare funding to include block grants for low-income families and tax breaks for businesses that help workers pay for daycare. Republicans oppose the amount as excessive.

- Several states are stepping to the plate with assistance programs of their own. This year Kentucky has provided some fifty million dollars in grants.

(It really is all about money. Many moms and dads, for that matter, cannot work because of the expense of daycare. Daycare centers are closing or are restricted on how they operate because of their costs which include payroll, utilities, mortgages, food and supplies, maintenance, insurance et al. One veteran daycare operator in Arkansas told the association that she earns $2 an hour after all her expenses are taken care of. She says she will not close, but things must improve. MLR)

God Bless America!

Made in the USA
Middletown, DE
25 June 2024

56232943R00116